Timelights

Timelights

Martin Edmond

99% Press,
an imprint of Lasavia Publishing Ltd.
Auckland, New Zealand

www.lasaviapublishing.com

Copyright © Martin Edmond, 2020

This book is copyright. Apart from any fair dealing for the purpose of private study, research, criticism or reviews, as permitted under the Copyright Act, no part may be reproduced by any process without the permission of the publishers.

ISBN: 978-0-9951282-8-6

Contents

1. The Old Country   9

    Dee Why Beach   13

    Bathroom Window   16

    Kitchen Window   19

    The Buddha of Featherston   22

    Rātana Cemetery   26

    Hotel Window   30

    Hall Windows   34

    Chateau Window   37

    Hot Pool   41

    Motel Window   45

    Esplanade Window   49

    Sedge   54

    Window with Cypress Tree   58

    Home Window   62

2. Golden Week — 67

Tokyo — 68
Kurohime — 77
Nojiriko — 86
Hokusai — 95
Mr T — 101
Snake and Fish — 110
Little Kyoto of the Snow Country — 120
Frog and Snake — 126
The Poet Issa — 129
Leaving Kumakura — 138

3. A Map of My Place — 143

Sitting Room — 149
Balcony — 154
Next Door Windows — 159
Study Window — 164
Bedroom Window — 169

Neighbours' Windows	174
Bathroom	179
When There Was Dust on the Window at 4 O'Clock	184
Empty Chair	189

A picture is worth a thousand words.

Anon

Caption: Latin captio-n, from capere 'take, seize'. 'Arrest' & 'warrant for arrest' gave rise to 'statement of where, when, and by whose authority a warrant was issued'; appended to a legal document, hence the sense 'heading or accompanying wording'.

Wicktionary

1

The Old Country

for Richard and Amala

Dee Why Beach

I went out to Dee Why to see Ken. It was a Sunday in January. A hot summer's day. We met in the Village Plaza, an old-fashioned, air-conditioned mall on Howard Avenue. Typically, I had come out with no hat and no sunnies and tried, unsuccessfully, to find one or the other or both to buy before Ken arrived: wearing shorts, an Akubra and aviator glasses. We went on down the avenue towards the beach, passing over some wide well-kept lawns where, he said, the local Tibetan community likes to gather for celebrations and devotions with their tents, their flags and their prayer wheels. Even though it was afternoon already, there was still a haze out to sea. We went bare foot, carrying our sandals, north along the ochre sands, talking. We are old friends but we don't see each other that often. We are also New Zealanders who met over here—a special category though who would know that? Or care. Anyway, north we went, across the ochre sands, in the hazy afternoon, towards the lagoon, talking about the old days and Mr Asia and the Calabrian mafia and what else I don't remember, our kids probably. It was when we were just about ready to turn around and go back that we came across the pole. Not far from the mouth of the lagoon. I don't rate myself as a photographer and I rarely take pictures—but this seemed to ask for it. And I am pleased with the result. After that, we caught a bus to Ken's place in Cromer Heights and drank some beers, ate a delicious green curry he made, had some glasses of wine, talked some more and listened to music; then, about 6.30 pm, I caught another bus into town. When I got home I went online to see what I could find out about the pole. Nada. Ken said later that his friend John Caves, a local identity, told him it is a marker set down in the 1960s to monitor the shifting sands of the dunes. There are two more, back of the strand, and several others out in the waters of the lagoon. These other poles are more shallowly anchored and can move, as the sands and the tidal waters move; while this one remains where it is and so may be used as a guide to measure the drift of the others. It reminded me of something I read years ago now, about the Irish-born American poet Lola Ridge. During her brief sojourn in Sydney in the early years of the twentieth century, a single mother, she lived out here with her young son in a boarding house which was in the process of being swallowed up by the sands. That ochre tide, encroaching upon their late colonial world, the closed doors and wooden verandas, the crinolines and the incipient despair, like something Edward Hopper might have painted. The unimaginable residents of that disintegrated place. Ken has a theory about the meaning of the name, Dee Why; but he's not yet ready to disclose it. He did let me read a brief account of it once however. It's persuasive, hallucinatory, just like that afternoon; and this would be a photograph of it if you could photograph a theory of a name; which of course you cannot.

Bathroom Window

It must have been the way afternoon light was falling in the window that caught my attention; those soft greens and fugitive reds, which probably represent the tree fern outside and the bricks of the adjoining apartment building. I can be more specific about the items on the sill. Far left, with the top knot and the shadow, is a figurine which comes from somewhere in the Pacific though I don't know exactly where. One of the island groups in Micronesia; perhaps the Carolines. A woman friend bought it for me from a dealer in antiquities she knew in Auckland. It's a puppet: the wooden legs articulate; the torso, made out of a piece of bone, is hollow; the arms, one of which has fallen off and, in the photo, sits behind, also articulate; the block of wood making up the head and shoulders,

with that wonderful top knot à la Grace Jones, comes off. It is said to have been a repository in which to store poisons used in black magic, which would be concealed in the hollow of the torso and reached by taking off the head piece, which closes the bone tube with a wooden plug. That bit of bone has a lizard carved in relief upon its back, with the tail disappearing between the figurine's legs and the head pointing up towards the nape of her neck. I've always thought it would be a good place to hide drugs, if I had drugs to hide. On the other side of the sill, harder to see, is a copy of the Venus of Willendorf which another woman friend gave me. It's made out of a smooth reddish stone, perhaps chalcedony, and has been constructed in such a way as to elide the surface features you find on the original; and feels good to heft in your hand. What's curious about these two figurines is that each resembles, in a general way, the woman who gave it to me: the one tall, slender, graceful, with small breasts and an upright stance; the other short, ample and curvaceous, though not as buxom, as the Venus. In between the two of them, in the centre, behind that pale green agate rock crystal standing up like a shark's fin, is a tiki in the Hawaiian style which I bought in a second hand shop in Manly in the days when I used to go over there once a week to get Chinese herbs from Tennyson Yiu to treat a liver infection I picked up in Fiji. It's made out of black coral and came along with a tiny copy, smaller than the tip of the little finger on a young girl's hand, also made of black coral, and designed to be worn on a chain around the neck. I gave it to a friend, Lud, who has since died. The three shells on the left were given to me, with a whole basket of other sea-shells, by a third woman friend who, I now realise, also resembles the Venus of Willendorf. The stones are from various places; most of the little ones I picked up on my daily ramble along Pearl Beach when I lived there in the 1990s; but that object you can just glimpse a part of on the far right of the picture is a piece of pumice which has been colonised by a marine creature, a worm probably, which built a maze of pink and white tunnels within and along its crumbly surfaces. I like the way the whole set-up looks like some sort of altar but an altar to what? To whom? Gaia in all of her many manifestations perhaps. Really, however, it's just a bathroom shelf, above the toilet, with the shower booth on the far side. And yet . . .

Kitchen Window

I took this photograph the night before we went away on holiday to New Zealand. I like going away but at the same time always feel reluctant to leave my apartment empty for any length of time, I don't know why, and I think that's why I took it—as a place-holder. It's of one of the two windows in my galley kitchen: the other, over the sink, looks out at the brick wall of the apartment building next door; this one faces west, past a small balcony, to the street and, beyond that, a view of receding red tile roofs, a couple of tall trees (a palm, a pine), culminating, as if in an Albrecht Dürer engraving, in the steeple of the neo-Gothic Anglican church of St Andrew on the corner of Smith and Henson Streets. Directly opposite me is the garden of a Pilipino man who is an assiduous and devoted

topiarist and likes to place among his carefully sculpted shrubs small plaster figures of birds, mainly, though there is also, beside his fountain, a statue of barefoot lovers, a yokel and his flower girl, under an umbrella. Of course you can't see any of that in the photo. And even the light, which might be assumed to be the moon, is actually a street-lamp which burns all night long on the telegraph pole across the road. When I look at the image I think of a passage from Italo Calvino's essay 'Exactitude', in which he quotes, at some length, remarks in praise of *il vago* made by Giacomo Leopardi; then writes: *Therefore Leopardi, whom I had chosen as the ideal opponent of my argument for exactitude, turns out to be a decisive witness in its favour . . . the poet of vagueness can only be the poet of exactitude, who is able to grasp the subtlest sensations with eyes and ears and quick unerring hands.* Both windows are curtained, the north-facing one with a piece of plain green gauze, this one with a section of russet cloth that has lime coloured lettering upon it reading: *Paris Louis Vuitton Paris Louis Vuitton Paris*, over and over. Those two indistinct dark reddish rectangular shapes you can almost make out on the right are, at the top, a laminated road map of Summer Hill I picked up one day in the street (it had been run over and still has bits of gravel impressed into the laminate) blu-tacked to the wall; and below that a rectangular wooden tray which I have never found a use for leaning upright against the tiles. As for that mysterious speck towards the bottom of the picture, that's a lamp which burns sometimes red, sometimes green, in the topiarist's garden. What I like about the image is the way the street-light resembles a flying saucer caught in a grid made by the wooden supports of the four panes of glass in each of the two sash windows; which I keep partly open, for the breeze, when I'm here but which I jam shut, using an old twelve inch school ruler, when I go away. Philip Larkin who lived, as I do, alone, wrote: *Home is so sad. It stays as it was left, / Shaped to the comfort of the last to go / As if to win them back. Instead, bereft / Of anyone to please, it withers* . . . but I <u>want</u> my home to stay as I left it so as to be here to please me when I return: *A joyous shot at how things ought to be,* Larkin says (disenchantedly) later in the poem. Yes, I say; exactly.

The Buddha of Featherston

We were in a Bed & Breakfast in Featherston called Bird Song Cottage. It was the morning of the ceremony and Amala and Richard were rehearsing the chants they would perform later on that day at the site of the old prisoner of war camp to the north of the town; while Mayu was recording them in case, because of the weather or for some other reason, she was unable to get good live sound in situ. I was just standing there reading along with the words when I saw sunlight slanting through the window of the cottage and projecting the shadow of the banister post onto a blue towel hanging over a wall heater at the base of the stairs leading up to the mezzanine. Of course the shadow of the post on the towel bears a resemblance to a person climbing the stairs; and may also, I suppose, be seen as a manifestation of the Buddha. We arrived at the farm at 11.00 am;

the farmer was waiting two thirds of the way down his driveway with a witch's hat behind him on the gravel, barring access to his house. He was a man of few words; we made our introductions then he pointed off to our right and said we could drive up the old central road and from there choose a place to perform our ceremony. I parked the car before a locked gate, we climbed over a fence and set out across a cow paddock towards a great tumulus of rubble made of bricks, concrete, barbed wire and other debris all bulldozed together; in the lee of which, upon a slab which had been the foundation of one of the prison huts, Richard and Amala, who was robed as a priest, chanted; while Mayu filmed and recorded and I bore silent witness. The incessant wind blew through long stalks of golden grass. In the west, beyond the ragged lines of the tops of windbreaks of pine and macrocarpa trees, the distant line of the Tararuas appeared and disappeared in the blue depth of the sky. A strange thing happened: I found I could read the texts of the chants without using my glasses, something I have not been able to do for more than twenty years now. After the chanting finished, Mayu spoke the names of the forty-eight Japanese POWs who died here in February, 1943; and also that of the single New Zealand guard killed by a ricocheting bullet. And as she spoke each name, it seemed that the ghost of the departed soldier wavered up from out of the earth and lingered for a moment in the bright air before blowing away. Afterwards, as we walked back to the car, I noticed that, among the twenty or so heifers in the paddock, there were two bulls, a Jersey and Friesian; but Richard, when we first arrived, had lain down in the grass in front of the herd and after that said we would not have any problem with the cattle; and we did not. When I told him how, during the chanting, the words on the page had suddenly come clear enough for me to read without glasses, he was inclined to see that as a further manifestation of the Buddha. His and Amala's practice is Zen, an apophatic theology: they say the Buddha's existence is in his non-existence; and, further, that in his non-existence is his existence. This too is apparent: the photo, with all of its many associations, in fact shows only a shadow falling upon a blue bath towel drying over a heater at 9.30 am on a sunny Monday, February 25, 2019, at Bird Song Cottage outside of Featherston in the Wairarapa.

Rātana Cemetery

We parked the car outside the temple and walked towards a large building on the square. Along the top of its wide veranda were models of all of the seven waka of the legendary Great Fleet, plus representations of Tasman's and Cook's vessels as well. The village seemed deserted but I could hear music playing: *I found myself a blue lady / To help me through the night.* Odd to hear Brazier's familiar voice booming out his self-consciously decadent lyrics in such a place. The Hello Sailor song was coming from a radio in a van from Marton which belonged to two workmen who were up on the roof of the tiny gymnasium making repairs. Next door to that, the locked building where all of the crutches, the wheelchairs and the walking sticks of those healed by the prophet are kept. No-one else around. When we went into the shop to ask if it

would be alright to visit the temple, the woman who shuffled out from the shadowy depths, although she gave us permission, seemed surly; and the man sitting on the steps, with a can of soft drink in his hand, turned his back to us. On a bench outside the temple, however, near where we'd parked, sat another man with a walking stick, toothless, cheerful and companionable. When the other fellow joined us I realised he was probably mute. The man with the stick said all the able-bodied were away at work, in a factory or at the freezing works or somewhere like that. He said the building next to the gymnasium was kept locked in order to sequester within the evil spirits who'd haunted the souls and / or bodies of those formerly afflicted. He said the temple is always open. He said go in. Even the prohibition upon the taking of photographs made him laugh. *They're all over the internet, nei!* The village of Rātana grew up as a shanty town built on the family farm by worshippers of the prophet after he proclaimed the first of his visions on November 8, 1919. It seems like an odd place for a town, on bare sloping ground open to the enormous sky, some distance from the sea; but T W Rātana had seen lightning descend from the heavens and strike the earth here. The neatly mown lawns were dry and golden, the suburban houses shuttered and deserted. Or were there silent people silently within? Where did their water come from? To the west, between two such houses, there was a small cemetery full of ornate tombstones, where members of the family of the prophet are buried. Mayu found a glove puppet, a lamb, on the road. A low hill rises to the north of the town and there the rest of the Rātana dead lie in serried ranks of joyously decorated graves: rainbow streamers, spirit catchers, plastic flowers of every colour and description; little plaster cats and dogs, children's toys, a framed letter to Santa; bottles of beer and packets of cigarettes; a tombstone cut into the shape of a football jersey and painted in the colours of the local team. Even a Japanese flag: Rātana, in 1924, visited that country and met with a Japanese Christian bishop who married a couple in his entourage, thereby giving rise to a story that the Māori and the Japanese peoples had also married each other; subsequently, the Hinomaru was sometimes flown over Rātana places. We wandered up and down the rows in the hot afternoon sun, feeling strangely moved by the exuberance of these graves as compared with the solemnity of those in the cemetery below. Afterwards we bumped back along the unsealed access road to the main drag then stopped the car a bit before the cattle stop so as to photograph the clock someone had fixed to the fence there. One of those electric clocks, ubiquitous in the 1960s and 70s on the walls of schoolrooms or government offices. I remember how the second hand would always pause momentarily, interminably, above the black dot marking each increment before lurching, with a tick, onwards to the next. This example, as you can see, is stopped at two minutes after seven. AM or PM, Pam quipped. I saw a hawk wheeling in the high blue sky; heard the whisper of wind in the macrocarpa trees at the turn off. Thistledown, barbed wire, a black and yellow AA sign with the words *Nga Puke Turua Urupa* written upon it, pointing away towards the end of time.

Hotel Window

There was a booking error so we ended up staying in the Governor's Suite at the Grand for the first few nights we were spending in Whanganui. It had a well-appointed sitting room with two leather couches; a polished wood dining table with eight chairs; a small water closet off that; at the other end, a bedroom with a king-sized bed and an ensuite. The art on the walls was bizarre: indistinct and fading prints of ersatz pre-Raphaelite or neo-Impressionist paintings. That first night I tossed and turned as if haunted by fragmentary dreams of an Imperium lost or abandoned by governors past. Neville, the owner, an eccentric and companionable fellow who restored old vehicles (a Studebaker bus; an MG sports car) and got around in shorts and jandals, told me that the provision of ensuites was, precisely, why this hotel survived when all of the

others of its ilk have not. Women prefer ensuites, he said. The vast and outré collection of prints, paintings, maps, posters and photographs on the walls of the various floors and in the rooms of the hotel was his. Charts of shipwrecks along the coasts of England, Scotland and Wales; photographs of sea planes and of naval accidents; portraits of famous sportsmen, mostly League or Rugby players; posters for Hollywood films (King Vidor's 1930 movie *Billy the Kid*); multiple weird Victorian images of cherubic children surrounded by puppies or kittens. A friend who'd also stayed there described the taste as 1970s Buggers' Baroque. I mostly used the water closet at the other end of the sitting room; disconcerted by the way water pooled on the linoleum floor during the night and yet was nowhere to be seen next morning. Where did it go? I considered informing the management but for some reason did not. Perhaps, I thought, Neville already knew. The Governor's Suite was on the second floor and faced east; early in the morning, if we had not pulled the curtains properly, shafts of yellow sunlight came scintillating through the gaps. Over the road were the Council Buildings, with a statue of John Ballance, Irish-born, newspaperman and colonial politician, on the corner. Across from that, a furniture store with faux Egyptian artefacts in the window and some old books which, when I inquired about them, turned out to be simulacra carved out of wood. Next door, a Salvation Army run second-hand bookshop where I found a hardback copy of Hector Bolitho's autobiography, *My Restless Years*: which, however, I did not buy, because it seemed that he had wilfully obscured the detail of the salacious life he'd led. He was in the entourage when the Prince of Wales, later Edward VIII, later still the Duke of York, made his notorious visit to Whanganui in 1920. Not long after that the Mayor, Charles Mackay, shot and wounded the young poet D'Arcy Creswell after Creswell, at the instigation of the RSA, tried to entice him into a homosexual honey trap. Bolitho, who was also gay, must have known about this but does not mention it in his book. There was an Irish Bar downstairs where, after their AGM, I talked to the historian of the local Rugby Union, a man who resembled a de-frocked priest; the only contentious item of business on the agenda, he said, was whether or not to include the 'h' in their name: Whanganui or Wanganui? They decided against it. After a couple of days the management moved us down a floor to a sunny corner room done out in wicker and blonde wood, 1960s English country estate style. This photograph of the east window of the sitting room in the Governor's Suite was taken on our last night there, after we'd been out to eat at a Japanese restaurant with a group of litterateurs who were in town to visit the places the writer Robin Hyde haunted during her sojourn in the city towards the end of the 1920s. It seems to look out upon mysteries which are, in the nature of things, also looking in upon us.

Hall Windows

It was July, 2004, fifteen years ago now. I came from the south with my two sons, Jesse aged 7, Liamh aged 4. We arrived about 3.30 on a clear winter afternoon and drove straight up the mountain. It had snowed on the weekend, the air was bright and cold, Ruapehu a dazzle of white against a blue sky. We threw snowballs at each other and made a snow dwarf, with no arms and one eye, on a small hill where the drifts were knee-deep; then, with red chafed hands and sodden feet, got back in the car and went down and checked in to the Mountain View Motel. There was a spa bath with mossy wooden surrounds in which we warmed ourselves up. That night, after Liamh had gone to sleep, Jesse asked if we could go for a walk. As soon as we stepped out the door, we heard music coming

from the Waimarino Brass Band hall opposite—a little old grey wooden building with a peaked roof and frosted windows which have lettering and notes of music painted on the glass. I had never heard music coming from there before. This was free-form, unclassifiable, but brass—certainly brass. As soon as we started walking towards the hall, however, the music stopped. When we reached the window, very quietly, I lifted Jesse—in his pyjamas, dressing gown and slippers—up so we could both look inside. In the centre of the hall, surrounded by a clutter of chairs and music stands, three people sat close together facing one another. Two men and a woman, young to middle-aged, wearing nondescript winter clothes. The men held a trumpet and a trombone, respectively; the woman, a French horn. They were leaning forward, deep in thought, not talking, as if communicating telepathically with each other. I put Jesse down and we tiptoed away. We went the other way and, on the corner of Burns Street and the Tohunga Road, in a small grassy gully, he pointed out a standing stone. It looked as if it had been placed there a long time ago; it looked like the kind of stone that might have a spiral carved onto it, a mauri stone perhaps. We saw it shining in the rainy night air under the light of five tall streetlamps. We could hear the Mangawhero, red river, beyond, and the other stream, the Mangateitei, high river, behind us: the old town was built at the confluence of these two rivers. We went back to check on Liamh, who was sleeping soundly, and then out again, this time to cross the road and hang over a white rail on the banks of the Mangateitei running below us through a stand of remnant beech forest, black water shifting beneath black trees. While we were there the music started up again. It was indescribably beautiful, an improvisation around a theme, structured like a raga, full of invention but in its feeling, shy, wild, and intimate. They played for about twenty minutes without stopping; we listened outside the hall until we got too cold then went back to the motel and listened from there. Jesse, who in those days often had trouble getting to sleep, dropped off while they were still playing. It was about half past nine on a Tuesday night. Slight rain drifted past the streetlamps. A big semi trailer with the word LILBURN on its side passed on the road, going north. Then another one that said COMMERCIAL. Though I haven't lived in Ohakune since 1962, I felt as if I had come home again at last.

Chateau Window

It was Sunday afternoon and we were sitting in the Ruapehu Room at the Chateau Tongariro having a drink. A glass of red, a syrah from Hawkes Bay, for me; a G & T for Mayu. She'd chosen from a variety of gins, and a variety of tonics, and seemed happy with the result. The cone of Ngauruhoe, bereft of snow, could be seen through the east-facing window. I wanted to photograph it but there were people sitting at the table and I didn't want to have to photograph them too. Eventually, when we were on to our second drink (an Australian shiraz for me, a different, celery-flavoured gin for Mayu, with a different tonic), they left, a waiter cleared the table and I took this shot. Later we walked out in the cold mountain air towards that bare volcanic peak. Toe toe flowered luxuriantly, creamily,

either side of the road; light from the westering sun flashed from the glossy spear-shaped leaves of the harakeke. Tongariro rose to the left; Ruapehu was on our right, a massive pile of purple rock, streaked with snow near the summit. To the north, in the distance, more peaks loomed black and miniature against the horizon: Maungatautari, Pirongia. We seemed to have been translated into another realm, to have become one with the sky people. Then, as we walked in the rapidly fading light back to the hotel, we came across a Department of Conservation sign that read: *Sewage Plant Road, No Exit*; which took some of the glamour away from the last rosy glow of the sun setting on those piles of magmatic extrusion. Or did it add something? In the restaurant we ate an excellent three course meal before descending into the bowels of the building to take a tepid bath in a pool which gave you an uncanny sense of being in the hold of a ship. It was the bolted metal plate white painted walls. Our room was towards the back of the hotel and gave out to a slope upon which grew native shrubs and trees. All night long I could hear the vast silence of the mountain looming through the window. I had never stayed there before. The year previous, though, while in the district, I'd visited, and bought, from a wood and stone carver who worked in a shed opposite the Chateau, an adze-shaped pendant, a toki, for Mayu. We'd thought of buying another, matching one this time but the shed was closed. Next morning, however, it was open; but when the hitherto silent man working therein brought out the toki for sale, there were only three remaining and none of them seemed quite right. He looked at the one Mayu was wearing and said it was made of totoweka, weka's blood. The man I bought it from told me he found the stone in a creek upon the mountain and carved it himself; but did not know what it was called. The Chateau was designed by Timaru architect Herbert Hall, who modelled the neo-Georgian structure, four storeys and a basement, upon a Canadian resort at Lake Louise near Banff in Alberta. It was built in the Depression by the Fletcher Construction Company using a work force of about eighty men, many of whom were recruited from nearby Waikune Prison. Now the staff come from all over and live, as the labourers used to do, in accommodation behind the hotel. We drove away down the mountain in the bright morning air with an odd feeling of regret, as if a kind of perfection, as displayed in that image of the volcanic cone framed in the window beneath a lighted chandelier, had been attained; only to be lost again immediately afterwards.

Hot Pool

The woman behind the desk at the Tokaanu Hot Pools said she would give us one of the cooler baths and handed over the key to Number 9. We didn't know why: did she think we looked too frail to handle the hotter ones? What's the point of a hot pool if it isn't hot? Anyway, we found the door, unlocked it and went inside; and then remembered we had no towels. Going back to hire some seemed too complex a procedure so we decided to do without; undressed and slid into the water. It was pleasingly warm and had the softness of soda, perhaps, or some other mineral; though in fact the waters are near enough to pH neutral. And the temperature range is small, 39-41 degrees centigrade, so there isn't much difference between the hot and the not so hot. Of course the water never seems quite as hot again as it does when you first get in; nevertheless, we could feel the

wai ora infiltrating itself into our muscles and bones which, if not exactly aged, are certainly no longer young. There's something erotic about being naked with your beloved in a hot pool in a closed room; on the other hand, you feel precluded from taking advantage of that privacy to indulge in love making because it is also in some sense a public space; or at least one used by others; so we confined ourselves to embraces, slinky soft skin against soft silky skin, tender kisses; as the twenty minutes we bought slowly, luxuriously and inexorably passed. Afterwards I waited on the bridge over the creek while Mayu went to the car to get changed. There were trout in the clear water below, their fins fibrillating, turning east to face the flow. They were of different sizes because this is a spawning ground. I became fixated upon a pair, one larger than the other, engaged in a complex dance, the smaller pursuing the larger, like lovers meeting and parting and meeting again. When Mayu came back we went for a walk through the thermal area, where there are scalding hot pools and boiling mud and even on occasion geysers, though none were playing on this day. I came here first as a child and when we saw an old wooden shed leaning in the scrub I thought I remembered what it was like in those far off days, when hot pools weren't lined with concrete but were simply holes in the ground full of water you climbed into. Then, in the mid-1970s, at Te Aroha, it turned out that the mud at the bottom of those pools harboured amoeba which could get up your nose and, by breeding upon the meninges, the membranes which enclose the brain, cause the sometimes fatal disease meningitis. I recall, too, coming here once on a school trip when I was a teenager: memories of cracking cold mornings and of the almost unbearable lure of a possible romance with one of the girls of our party; which never occurred or should I say occurred only in my imagination; and, who knows, perhaps also in hers. This photo suggests seclusion but also surveillance: those three and a bit windows along the top of the picture, built to allow light into the enclosed room, make you think of eyes or at least of places through which prying eyes might look: at two aging people, not cavorting together, but holding themselves sweetly and tenderly in each other's arms.

Motel Window

The motel was called Sails on the Lake and designed after a vague and unpersuasive nautical theme: shades like canvas, blue and white paint, slatted, laddering, wooden structures. Mayu found it online after we'd lunched in town; we were Auckland bound but didn't wish to drive any more that day. After the tall and faintly intimidating Scandinavian woman with a New Zealand accent (or vice versa) checked us in, we went down to the lake for a swim. The water was clear and cool and shallow for a long way out. Mayu waited on the shore while I waded until it was deep enough to dive, did a few strokes of freestyle then floated on my back and looked away south. There, in the distance, on the other side of the lake, I could see the mountains we'd left behind that morning: Tongariro, Ngauruhoe, Ruapehu; and before them graceful

Pīhanga, shaped like a breast and, in the legend, female and an object of contention and desire among the male mountains surrounding her. It was near there we'd had the hot pool; now I was bathing in the pellucid waters which fill the caldera of one of the world's largest volcanoes. The Taupō ryolitic super volcano began erupting 300,000 years ago; the Oruanui eruption, a Great Year past, is responsible for the present shape of the lake; the Hātepe event of 232 CE its most recent eruption. It blows up every thousand years or so; the 1800 years since the last explosion is not as long as the 3000 year gap between 8100 and 5100 BC. When she saw a lithe, athletic woman come down to the lake's edge, disrobe and swim out towards where I was, Mayu decided to join me in the water. Not that she had anything to worry about. We drifted companionably back to the pumice-strewn shore together. We had on our travels become obsessed with Caesar salads and especially with the recent propensity for restaurants to leave out the anchovies: which we thought indispensible. Everywhere we went we asked if they still made them, with the cos lettuce, the bacon, the croutons, the halved soft boiled eggs . . . and the anchovies. At one place the waiter sniffed and said: *It's in the dressing.* Here in Taupō we found a restaurant that did takeaways and still prepared the dish the old way; even though it turns out the Italo-Mexican chef who invented it himself abjured the use of anchovies. When he first made the salad, from scratch, after a rush at the Cesar Hotel in San Diego on July 4, 1924, he said the fishy taste came from Worcestershire sauce. I bet the

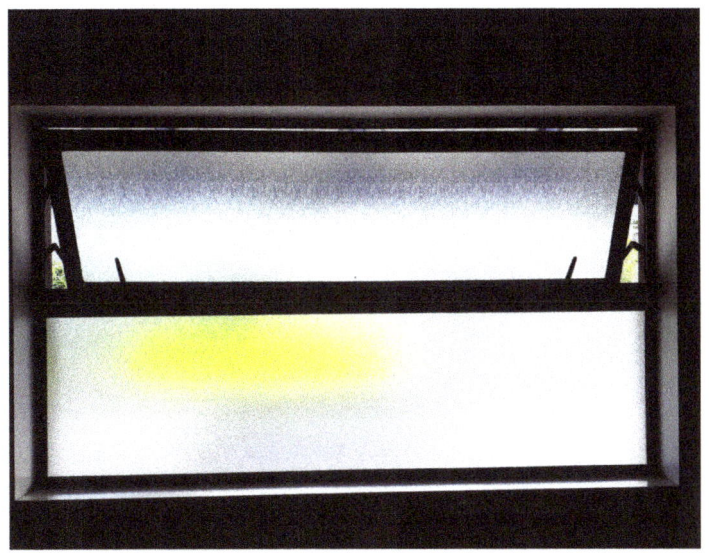

fancy chefs don't use that any more either. Or maybe they do. Anyway, that's what we had for dinner. Two servings, actually. Then we ran a spa bath that was as hot, or hotter, than we could ever have wished it to be; so much so that when we got out I lay down and fell asleep and didn't wake up until morning came. While we were packing up to go we couldn't find the i-phone charger and, looking to see if it had fallen under the bed, I spied a dark lumpy shape and reached in to draw out someone's crumpled black lace knickers, apparently discarded during a moment of passion and then forgotten. I carried them between thumb and forefinger to the rubbish bin, not without wondering what the Scandinavian New Zealander (or vice versa) might think when or if she found them. The photo is of the bathroom window at the back of the unit, snapped just before I closed and locked it. Both banal and intriguing, it suggests some kind of portal through which alien knowledge might come. Or go. As for a Great Year, that is *the period of one cycle of the equinoxes around the ecliptic*; about 25,800 years; after which the stars return to where they were before. For those 'fixed' stars we see in the night sky are not really fixed, they turn, as everything turns. Which means the brightest of the circumpolar stars currently visible in the southern sky, Miaplacidus (placid waters) in the constellation Carina (the Keel) in the past was not where it is now; and in the future will not be there either; until another Great Year passes. I imagine the caldera will have erupted again, many times, before that happens.

Esplanade Window

Ever since I worked as a lighting roadie for Coup D'Etat and The Pink Flamingos in the early 1980s, I'd wanted to stay a night or two at the 'Splade, as we called it, a venue we played in Devonport; and now I was. But the long elegant auditorium in which those two bands repeated their louche, delirious, half-forgotten songs (*Allende! In my Chevrolet*) seems to have disappeared; made over into apartments I think. Our rooms were upstairs, on the corner, facing out towards the ferry terminal: a white-painted bathroom as big or bigger than the bedroom with a ceiling fan which turned lazily, silently, all night long in the sticky March heat. On our first night we went across the road to the library for the launch of the *Poetry New Zealand Yearbook* and there I bumped into Bob Orr. Bob

was returning to Te Mata, where he lives, in the morning; but suggested we meet up at the Sierra Café in the terminal for a coffee before he did so. We were going on the 11.00 am ferry to Waiheke Island to visit my sister Frances so I thought a 9.30 rendezvous would give us plenty of time to talk; but there was no sign of Bob in the terminal and no Sierra either, though there was one up on the main drag. We went back and forth twice before I realised he must have meant the Sierra over the water at the city terminal at the bottom of Queen Street in Auckland. I tried phoning but no luck. By then it was too late to go across; and melancholy to think of him sitting there waiting for us on the other side of the harbour upon which his working life had been spent. Later he wrote that he waited about an hour and didn't really mind: *it was quite pleasant watching ferry boats and their passengers coming and going and reflecting on all those years I too plied every day those very same waters.* I was going to tell Bob about the date we had later in the week out at Hobsonville to see a nineteenth century wooden schooner, the *Daring*, recently emerged, after heavy tides, from the black sand of the dunes where she was buried, in 1865, on the wild west coast north of Muriwai not very far from the mouth of the Kaipara harbour. The invitation came from a maritime historian who learned that the *Daring*'s owner, a rogue Scotsman and embezzler called David Kirkwood, subsequently carried, on another of his ships, a Japanese circus from Yokohama to San Francisco and back again and he thought Mayu might be interested in that; as indeed she was. The Great Dragon Troupe also toured New Zealand and Australia in the late 1860s and early 1870s: pole equilibrists, a paper rope walker, the butterfly trick man, clowns, tumblers and acrobats, top spinners, trapeze artists, jongleurs and illusionists. The rain was pelting down in Hobsonville. The *Daring*, built in 1863 on the beach at Mangawhai, stood upright in a stout wooden cradle under a canopy of white plastic sheeting and seemed an enormity, its great kauri beams supported by elbows of pōhutukawa sawn directly from the tree and with bark still adhering to them; its hull lined with brass coppering; its ballast stones and rusted anchor chain spilling from a box outside the entrance to the canopy. It will in time be restored, but only to the state it was in when found again; that is, before local souvenir hunters had been at it with their chainsaws. The Esplanade was built later, in 1903, and now belongs to Chinese investors who also own hotels in Melbourne, Perth, Kuala Lumpur and who knows where else. It was modelled on Edwardian waterfront promenade hotels in English resort towns, specifically one of the same name at Brighton, and is heritage listed for its façade, parapets, plasterwork, urns and double-hung sash windows. The leadlight glass in the stairwell shimmered in the silvery late afternoon sun but I couldn't get a decent shot of it; at night I became fascinated by the sporadic comings and goings in the street outside, where Queens Parade meets Victoria Street. Nothing untoward occurred; but still. The true mystery, after all, lies not in the event itself but in what might be about to happen;

or in what has just happened; or indeed in what never really happens at all. Or so this photo seems to suggest.

Sedge

On Sunday afternoon we left where we were staying, at Peter's place in Favona, and drove over to Onehunga to see Richard. Amala wasn't going to be there, she was at the Zen Centre all day long. Their house, on the eastern shores of Manukau Harbour, overlooks a small reserve where, it is said, Te Whero Whero, later Pōtatau, the first Māori King, built a whare in 1843. Richard invited us in, showed us around and then made tea: a small lump of vegetable matter, which he took from a coloured, compartmentalised box, opened up, in the hot water of the glass pot, to reveal an exotic flower whose essence we drank. He and Mayu were exchanging information and needed to link their computers so that the data might flow unimpeded from one to the other. It consisted of still photographs, moving pictures and sound files gathered during

the time we'd spent in Featherston ten days before. Once they were set up, we left the machines to their own devices and went for a walk. Down Normans Hill Road, along Beachcroft Avenue then, via a pedestrian bridge, over Hugh Watt Drive to Taumanu Reserve, where an artificial beach has been laid and landscaped. We passed a lagoon, the Onehunga Bay Reserve, also man-made, on our right before we reached Taumanu; there, arcane water sports were in progress: some combination of skate boarding and obstacle jumping, with attendant loud speaker announcements to the lycra-clad and insignia-festooned participants. Dogs swim in the waters of the lagoon, Richard said, but not humans. Onehunga was in 1847 proclaimed New Zealand's first fencible settlement. Over 800 retired British soldiers and their families, also known as Fencibles, were given land grants by Governor Grey and, along with a group of 121 Ngāti Mahuta warriors contributed by Te Whero Whero, made up the military defence of Auckland against possible attack by hostile tribes to the south. Both groups were commanded by British officers; each supplied their own weaponry. In time, of course, Pōtatau Te Whero Whero ended up on the other side; but he was spared knowledge of the theft of his ancestral lands by his sometime friend, George Grey, *that terrible and fatal man*, because he'd already died, in 1860, before the invasion of the Waikato took place. Ancient history which, on this reclaimed land, where we walked down concrete paths between municipal gardens, seemed still to be alive. I took a photograph of a bank of grass, with blue sky above, but inadvertently left a finger over the edge of the aperture so there was a dark smudge at the top right hand corner of the image. It's one of the few photos I've cropped. I like the tumult of green and gold stems, the white fragments of shell lying on the pale ground beneath. Later a landscape gardener told me it's called Oioi, a sedge whose botanical designation is *Apodasmia similis* and common name *jointed wire rush*. The Māori means *to sway gently* and refers to the way, as here, the grass moves in the wind. It likes to grow on the edges of tidal rivers and lakes and in sand on damp sea flats; around peat bogs and hot springs. A Gondwanaland plant: related species grow in South Africa, Australia and South America. It's probably, like the tuatara, old as the dinosaurs; and was used for thatching on the rooves of houses; perhaps even upon the roof of Te Whero Whero's whare. Avoiding prams, bicycles and other humanimals, we crossed a second bridge over the motorway and walked back to the house, where we found that those excellent and obedient machines had finished their colloquy and so supplied Mayu and Richard with copies of each others' files. Then, after an inconclusive discussion of the meaning of the name Favona, we took our leave and drove back to Pete's place, opposite a vast corrugated iron Samoan church, resounding with song this Rātapu in that enigmatic suburb.

Window with Cypress Tree

The sitting room looked southwest through a line of cypress trees growing very close to the house. I took some shots of the windows but in the end kept only this one, of the skinny right hand pane. The green is vivid, even hallucinatory; with which the browns of the bark make a pleasing contrast; while the slight lean in the composition reminds me of a Philip Clairmont painting. I mean a specific work: *Self portrait in a Butterfly Mirror* (1978), not one of my favourites. He pictured himself trapped in the centre panel of an elongated dressing table mirror with related apparitions in both side panels. The acid greens, the bright blues, the reds out of which the painting is made give me a sense of tipping chaos, a nausea like that which you feel during an attack of motion sickness. For some people, of course, this is true of all of his works; but I continue to seek the still point, the place of tranquillity, which seems to be lacking in this work but might yet turn out to be there. As always with Phil's painting, it's worth going in for a closer look. The face in the mirror, reminiscent of the one in Munch's *The Scream,* is like a pleading ghost. It also resembles an upright light bulb whose filament is going to blow; whose globe is about to shatter. It is surrounded, as mentioned, by alternate selves, some jaunty, some malevolent, some enraged, some merely insouciant; in amongst passages of paint that are both abstract and beautiful. As if that is where true felicity might be found. It's the acidulous green makes me ill; while the green of the cypress tree in the photo makes me feel the opposite: warm, welcome, perhaps even home, if by that we understand at home in the world. Colour is, after all, emotional. And, as has been noted before, *we have a relationship with the colour green*. The other resemblance between this image and the Clairmont is that in each we see a shape like a flame, or flames, rising. Green flames. *The force that through the green fuse drives the flower*. Cypress trees do indeed look like flames; emanations rising from the ground into the air. And, if photographed in the right way, will disclose an envelope of spectral energy, like a membrane, around the solidity of leaf and branch. If you've ever seen Kirlian photographs you'll know what I mean. Here there are perhaps analogies with the Chinese concept *chi*, the energy which animates all living things. That's a lot to load on a photo of a tree outside a window. Or not. No matter, never mind. I confess I do not know. I am one who can entertain any idea, without ever making a commitment to a single system of belief. That is perhaps why perhaps is one of my favourite words. Also I have a head full of lines of poetry, typically divorced from context. *Green, green, I love you green / Green wind, green branches / The ship upon the sea / And the horse upon the mountain.* That's Lorca. It was the last day of our holiday. We packed up and, later on, caught a plane to Sydney. Outside my place, by the letter box, after we took our luggage from the boot of the taxi and were going inside, Elaine told us that the half grown black and white cat, Brodie, who had a personality as large as a house, was run over last week. His envelope of energy, his chi, dispersed into the ether. I told her of the old belief, that all cats are Egyptian and furthermore there is a finite number of cat souls abroad in the world at any one time: so that every cat is a reincarnation of another cat; which means that Brodie will, sooner or later, come back to us. I could not tell if this left her consoled, unconsoled or inconsolable.

Home Window

This photograph was taken before we went away but I didn't find it on my phone until after we came back. That's my dining room table under the west facing window in the twilight of another Sydney day. On the right you can just see half a dozen white pillars of what a friend called my Abba balcony—go figure—while the sliver of grey behind that is the side of a building which used to belong to an undertaker and is now the home of an IT guy, his wife and their five children. In the centre of the image, behind the Venetian blinds, you can just glimpse, against the pale sky, the top of a very tall palm tree which seems to be dying. With its vestigial, drooping head and outflung fronds it always makes me think of the composition of Gauguin's *Yellow Christ*; but the predominant colour here is of course green. Again. There was a pink flowering hibiscus out

the open window, a variety called Suva Queen; it's since been pruned, severely. Someone's car over the road. Another friend commented: all it needs is a profile of Robert Mitchum; to which I replied he's probably in there somewhere. Sitting in the chair to the left perhaps. Laurie might have been referring to any of the noir films Mitchum appeared in in the decade after the war; or, more likely, to the 1975 picture *Farewell, My Lovely*, after the Raymond Chandler novel. Or maybe the 1978 version of *The Big Sleep*, in which Mitchum also played detective Philip Marlowe, although this time the action was shifted from Los Angeles to London. So why not inner city Sydney towards the end of the second decade of the third millennium? Slightly earlier in the evening, that tree you can see the trunk and lower branches of on the right, a tallowood, would have played host to a gang of rainbow lorikeets. They gather there towards the close of day, in the bare branches of the crown, which have been stripped naked by their activities, to talk over their concerns. I have tried to work out what they are saying. I have watched them closely, their pirouettes and arabesques. Pairs of them frequently join beak to beak, tongue to tongue, as if exchanging saliva or perhaps nectar. They flirt together: one will hang upside down by a single claw, swinging back and forth like an acrobat upon a trapeze, while the other perches up above on the same branch, staring as if in fascination down at this performance. And so on. All of their antics are accompanied by loud, abrasive squawking which is, I must admit, hard upon the ears. They go on like this for about twenty minutes, during which time some pairs, their vocabulary of squawks apparently exhausted, will fly away into the east; while others, almost always from the west, fly in to join the conversation. It must be some song of themselves they are singing. Some sort of parroting only parrots parrot. Then, when the last pair has gone, silence descends and the shadows gather in that noir way you see in the indistinct areas of the photograph, which makes my place look far more enticing and mysterious than it actually is. Or not. A faint gleam of fruit in the fruit bowl, that strip of lacquered table top, the stones, which you cannot see, lying along the window sill. One of them, a favourite, is a small black pebble, smooth and oval shaped, I bought in a shop in Labuanbajo on the Indonesian island of Flores in 2004 for a fantastic sum of money: 150,000 rupiah perhaps; which, after all, is only about $15.00 and might have been even less back then. I remember how the owner, an old woman, cackled with delight when she realised I was actually going to pay good money for something as worthless as a stone; also how she refused absolutely to bring the price down by a single rupiah. Perhaps the true mystery is why I had to have that particular pebble which, however, I've never regretted buying and still consider a jewel beyond price. It's there, on the left of the image, under the strut which makes the vertical of a ghostly cross that seems to have the car outside in its sights. See?

2

Golden Week

for Mayu

Tokyo

We landed at Haneda Airport at 5.00 am. It was raining and everything seemed veiled in grey. Coming through Customs was like crossing over a *cordon sanitaire*; I felt as if my DNA, along with my passport, was being scrutinised. Immigration gave me three months; the visa, a stamp with perforated edges gummed down onto the page, shows a green and white Mt. Fuji and the outline of a five-petalled flower: *sakura*, cherry blossom. In the terminal young women were re-doing their lipstick using mobile phones as mirrors. Nondescript men lay stretched out sleeping on benches. Mayu queued, waiting for a store to open so she could buy a Subscriber Identification Module card. I went to get a coffee. Confused by the signage, I ordered a mocha, something I'd never done before. Sugar, chocolate, cream, syrup, marshmallow but

no coffee. I had to wait until Mayu arrived before I could add caffeine to the sugar rush. Then we caught a bus into town. Industrial buildings lined dark canals in the still falling rain. The muted colours of a northern city. Blues and ochres. That indefinable sense of the foreign in every single piece of design, including the power poles with their transistors and insulators and gleaming wires. Trees along the avenues, tortured into bizarre, truncated shapes, were just coming into leaf. From Shinjuku interchange we caught a cab to Mayu's mother's place in Yoyogi, *tree of generation*. The back left hand side doors of Japanese taxis open and close automatically and it is a mistake to try to work them manually. In the laneway outside the building, a blaze of purple from a bank of flowering azaleas.

Mioko, Mayu's sister, was about to go on a business trip to Hong Kong. They hugged and kissed and talked until it was time for her to leave. 8.11 am. We lay down for a while on Mioko's bed; I took a photo of the curtain over her door. Then we went by train to Aoyama, *blue mountain,* where Mayu's hairdresser has her salon on the fifth floor of a building opposite the Spiral Gallery. She ascended by lift and, while she was having her hair done, I walked down Omotesando, the Pilgrim's Way, to the Meiji Shrine at the bottom of the hill. It's a fashionable part of town. Lined with zelkova trees, the Japanese elm, also coming into leaf. In a shop window a circle of handbags was arranged like a target upon a wall; the one in the middle exploded and its heart-burst spattering blood red over the bags around about it. I went into the Oriental Bazaar, a famous shop, and looked at a series of prints showing women at the baths. A fight, typically between two older women, would always be breaking out left of centre of the wide steamy scene; the reverberations spreading, like waves, through the rest of the room. The Meiji Shrine is dedicated to the deified spirits of Emperor Meiji (1852-1912) and Empress Shōken (1849-1914) and commemorates their opening up of Japan to the West in 1868. It was built during and after World War One over the site of an iris garden the imperial couple liked to visit. A national project, mobilizing people throughout the land, who contributed time, labour and money. The original buildings were destroyed by Allied bombing in World War Two; the present version completed rebuilding in October, 1958. You walk down wide gravelled avenues, beneath enormous carved wooden arches made out of cedar logs, through evergreen forest: seventy hectares containing, they say, 120,000 trees of 365 different species, donated from all over the archipelago. Crowds of people passed by, both *gaijin* and not. At the Naien, the inner precinct, pilgrims, some in traditional dress, lined up to sprinkle themselves with sacred water. Gaijin men were ignoring signs that forbade photography; when rebuked by monks, they took no notice. I heard the harsh single *caw* of the Japanese crow sounding overhead. Sometimes their heavy bodies crashed down upon a perch in the branches of a pine tree. In Ura-Harajuku tiny boutiques overflowed with goods in laneways full of jostling crowds. There was a Brazilian television crew, a stylish young woman presenter talking to camera. Another young woman came out onto the balcony of

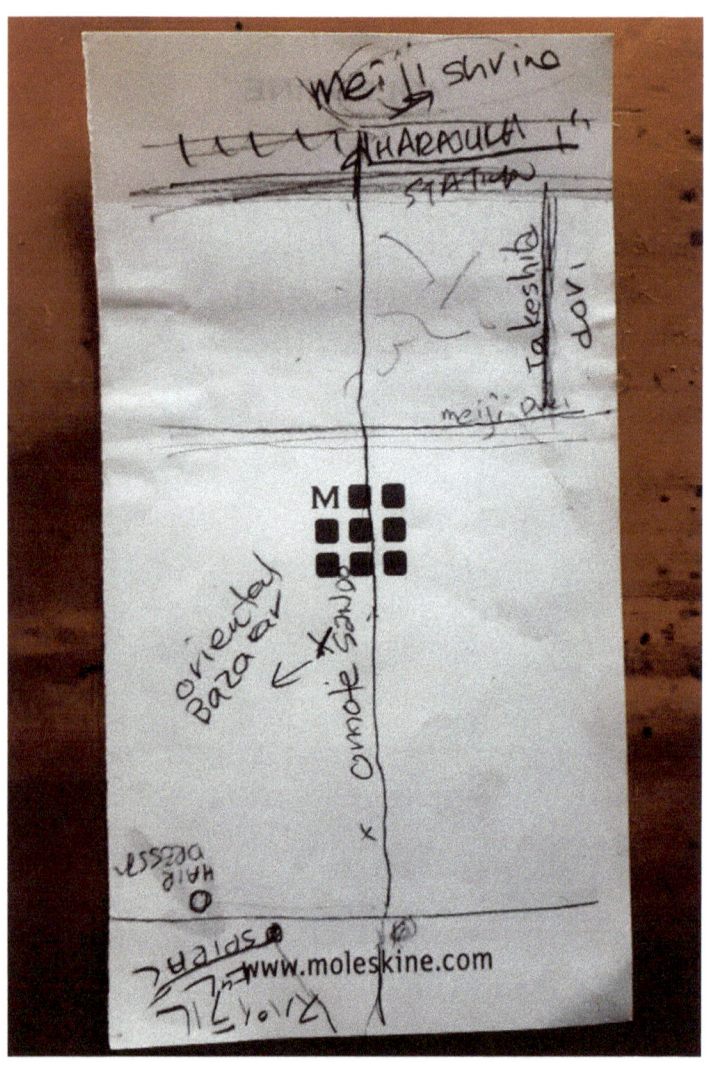

a sweet shop holding in her hands a mound of pink candy-floss shaped like a pagoda twice the size of her head. There was a shop with *No Sex Services* written across its window. Everything inside was also pink; it took me a while to realise that was the actual name of the business; but I never worked out what they sold. Sex toys perhaps. Mayu had drawn me a map, I followed it back up the other side of the Pilgrim's Way. Smartly dressed, immaculately coiffed and made-up women clipped past in their high-heeled shoes; they favoured long, diaphanous dresses falling to their calves; so unlike the short skirts and tights and tank tops of the punky girls on Cat Street. I went along Aoyama Street to the Spiral Gallery, where there was a show of 1960s Japanese Pop Art about which I recall nothing at all.

In the shop on the mezzanine there were kits of cut-out card from which to construct giraffes, pandas and zebras; tiny intricate models of famous aeroplanes like the Kitty Hawk and the Spirit of St Louis; miniature bicycles made out of steel wire; and compasses in round embossed leather wallets showing the way to navigate maps of countries that have not been discovered yet. Some of the displays were laid out upon the pages of English language books of surprising provenance: de Quincey's *The English Mail Coach*. Gray's translation of Dante's *Inferno*, Canto XXXIII, the Ugolino story. Many different kinds of stationary: for note-taking, for the writing of messages of love or condolence. Pens and pencils; inks made out of soot and animal glue, with incense or medicinal herbs added to give olfactory pleasure during the act of writing or reading. I bought a card with the silhouettes of seventeen black cats upon it for Mayu's mother; the packaging—envelope, paper bag—as discreet and elegant as Yoshie herself turned out to be.

Mayu had to go up to her bank in Roppongi, *six trees*. The trees, alas, are no longer there; the last, a 600 year old gingko, was destroyed by bombing during the war. Or they may have been *keyaki*, the Japanese name for the zelkova. Another version of the origin of the word Roppongi is that six families of courtiers lived here during the time of the Tokugawa Shogunate, all of whom had surnames which included the word *ngi*, 'tree'. A third suggests this was once a pine forest where wood-getters from Edo, down below, came for timber. Now developers are re-planting trees along the boulevards. The bank was upstairs, reached by way of a lift. People sat waiting for their number to be called by one of the immaculate tellers sitting behind perspex screens on the other side of the room. They approached the counter, stated their business, and were given another number; while the teller went away to transact whatever business it was. To the right, beneath cloudy windows, two queues of people lined up before machines where cash deposits could be made. It was Friday afternoon; at 4.00 pm the banks would close for Golden Week; they wouldn't open again for another ten days. Mayu was requesting a statement; which they (a branch of Mitsubishi Corporation) refused to give her unless she came in person and brought proof of address. This was complicated by the fact that, in Mayu's case, it was her mother's address she had to give. Did she or did she not live with her mother? Yes, while in Japan, she did. Even so, the bank seemed unsure if they should, could, or would provide her with the information she wanted about how much money there was in her own account. Mayu is usually a calm person but the slowness of the service, the stupidity of the task, the bloody-minded institutionalised procedural unhelpfulness of the staff, soon made her irate. When we were done at last, and leaving, a woman came out of an anonymous door with one more query: did they have her mother's address written down correctly? It was like something that might have happened in a small New Zealand town in the 1950s. Afterwards we went to a bar for a glass of wine and a snack. At the next table, a group of Argentineans were drinking beer and watching soccer on TV. Roppongi is the district where Mayu lived aged nine to eighteen years. That's why her bank is here. She knows these streets, their bars and restaurants, their clubs and gambling joints, like the back of her hand. Their diplomatic residences. She said it is a different place at night. I saw her as a young girl, dutiful, solemn and unafraid, walking home from the American School through streets where soldiers came for R & R. When we left the bar the rain had cleared, the big neon advertising signs on the main drag were coming on, the street lamps too, and, as we descended into the mouth of the subway to return to Yoyogi, in the murk and prescience of the early evening air, Tokyo resembled the once and future city in *Bladerunner*; until I remembered that it is actually the city in *Bladerunner* which resembles Tokyo. We ate that night in a *yakatori-ya*, a chicken restaurant around the road from Yoshie's flat. Behind a low bar the kitchen staff prepared a succession of tasty dishes which I tried and failed to memorise. I was drinking red wine. Each new glass came out of the cupboard in a plastic bag which had been placed around it after it had been removed, steaming, from the dishwasher. The glass was wiped with a fresh cloth before the wine was poured. Mayu, however, drank sake. The chef and his assistants, a teenage boy with a paper mask over his mouth and nose, a vivacious young woman, were joined by a third, another young woman; perhaps they were all related to each other in some way. In the tiny space, the four of them improvised the choreography of an intricate dance; while at the bar, a businessman in a suit drank beer after foaming beer from big glass tankards; and ate plate after plate of grilled chicken, all the while turning, fiercely it seemed, the pages of a *manga*.

Kurohime

It was snowing when we arrived at Kurohime station. Big soft flakes drifted like fractals in the grey afternoon air. Yoshie couldn't drive to meet the train because of the weather; she sent her boyfriend instead. There he was, short and stocky, bowing and smiling when we came through the narrow door from the platform into the railway station office. The appellation 'boyfriend' is ironic but that doesn't mean it isn't accurate too. He used to be Yoshie's second husband's drinking companion. Now he takes her out on excursions in his little truck. And that was how he took us, through bare unfenced fields of tilled black earth, along the narrow ways of a village whose house doors opened directly onto the road, through gardens of blue grape hyacinths, yellow daffodils and red tulips, past drifts of impacted snow, to a house built on the bank of a rushing river,

swollen at this time of year by the spring melt. Amidst larch and birch trees coming into leaf, pine and cedar, an understory of bear bamboo. Akagawa means red river; you turn off the road to Yoshie's place after crossing Bridge Number Three, which has attached to its low sides four separate metal plaques, two on each parapet, documenting the construction of the bridge. There is a power pole just to the left of the entrance to her driveway which, because it was at the time of building the last house on the road, Yoshie paid for herself. Now residents further up the mountain give her an annual rental for the right to use it as well. She is in her eighties. A lithe slender woman with a long head and a gracious manner. Somewhat stern, indeed imperious. It was still snowing, so her boyfriend didn't linger, staying just long enough for a greeting and a photograph; it turns out he has not entered the house since Yoshie's husband died some years ago. It was warmed by a small stove in the corner of the sitting room, and in the *tatami* room there was the *kotatsu*, a low table with an electric heater below where, sitting on cushions on the floor with our legs dangling down underneath, we ate the meal Yoshie prepared for us. She doesn't speak much English, just a word or two; and I didn't speak any Japanese; so I just listened to the music of the conversation between mother and daughter. They were arguing, not in any heated manner. Yoshie offered to give up her own bed for us; but Mayu didn't want to sleep with the cats' kitty litter which, while kept fastidiously clean, nevertheless stood on the floor at the end of her mother's bed. There were three cats, a tortoiseshell female who belonged to Yoshie and two neutered toms, one tabby, the other ginger, who were Mioko's. All three of these cats were exceptionally shy. In the end, Mayu prevailed and we slept in the tatami room, on futons pulled out of the big built-in wardrobe with sliding screens, *shoji*, to one side; under blankets and eiderdowns and doonas; with the shoji leading to the rest of the house left open just wide enough for a body to slip through sideways when one or other of us needed to go to the bathroom in the night. Even though the river was on the far side of the house I could still hear its running waters, just as I used to be able to hear, as a child, the rushing waters of another red river, the Mangawhero, on the slopes of another volcano, Ruapehu, a hemisphere away from Kurohime in Aotearoa. I slept, as they say, like a baby.

◈

The weather cleared overnight and when I woke up next morning and looked out the window, past the paper blinds, I saw something that I could not at first construe. A vast silver inflatable, or dome, that was somehow suspended in the sky above the trees. The mountain snapped into focus without banishing that strangely alien first vision. Kurohime means *Black Princess*; but, in keeping with other Japanese words, each of which has, as it were, a ghost companion, it can also mean *Secret Iron*. This district, Shinano, was known in the old days for its forges and blacksmiths, and for the weaponry and agricultural implements they made here.

The mountain was the home of a dragon, a shape shifter who, in the guise of a handsome young samurai, won the heart of the daughter of a local lord. But the lord set the suitor many tasks to do before he would give his daughter's hand in marriage; and even after the samurai completed all of them, still her father would not give up the princess. The samurai reverted to dragon shape (some say he became a giant snake) and laid waste to the land with fire and water; until everybody pleaded with him to stop. The price was that the princess had to go and live with him on the black mountain; she did; and there, it is said, they still

are. Kurohime is one of five volcanoes standing on the shores of an ancient caldera called Nojiriko. This mountain, and some of the others too, seemed to give forth a white light from within. Common sense says that must have been an effect of sunshine reflecting off snow; but that was not what it looked like. Rather it seemed that a central core of timelight buried in the heart of the mountain was streaming upwards, illuminating the clouds above with its silver rays.

Over breakfast Yoshie and Mayu discussed the plan for the day. The scheme they negotiated was shopping followed by lunch followed by a visit to a hot pool—*onsen*—then a return home to cook the delicacies that had been purchased or gathered for dinner. With detours to visit museums, shrines, temples and other places of interest, this was the routine—shopping, lunch, onsen, shopping, dinner—we followed for the rest of the week. At 10.00 or 11.00 every morning we would climb into the sleek black BMW 2105 sedan parked out the front of the house and set off for the day; returning in the late afternoon to embark upon preparations for the evening meal. At a market in Nakano, Yoshie bought fresh vegetables harvested that morning from local farms. There was a communal basin full of miso soup at the back of the shop, men, women and children sitting round about it on wooden benches, ladling the soup into bowls and drinking it. More was cooking out the back, so that the big basin was constantly being replenished. The soup was fragrant and spicy and gave me a sense that I was drinking in the goodness of the earth. Next we went to a bigger, swisher supermarket in the nearby city of Nagano for more supplies. Yoshie is a careful shopper; she would examine a particular tomato for ages before replacing it and choosing another one. She likes clams, so there were packets of those wrapped, as everything was wrapped, in plastic. Even the soft sweet bread she bought was wrapped in several layers of plastic. When I remarked upon this Mayu said:

Yes; but when it goes, it will all go. Lunch was in a small Chinese place at the side of the road; one of Yoshie's favourites. Because she had a driver this week (me, later Mioko) she was re-visiting all the places she likes best. Yoshie has been coming to Kurohime— real name Kumakura, 'Bear's Larder'—since 1974 when, after her divorce from Mayu's father, she used her alimony to buy a place on the other side of town from where her house is now.

The onsen was on the slopes of Myoko, the volcano next to Kurohime; its profile oddly reminiscent of that of Ruapehu. We drove through the narrow streets of resort towns built in the 1960s and now in a state of evocative disrepair. You could imagine a noir movie unfolding within their olive green and dull ochre interiors, where impeccably gloved staff remain inscrutable in the shadows as a desperate plot thickens. Or thins. The denouement takes place in one of the hot pools, a body face down in the water, the black blood ballooning out like a tumour, wisps of steam curling off the green water. Onsen etiquette says that you must strip naked and sit on a low stool before a mirror, washing yourself all over with a cobra tap that you hold in your hand, before entering the pool. You leave your big towel behind, to dry yourself with later, and take with you a small hand towel. With this you may rinse yourself; wipe the sweat from your brow; or, soaked in cold water, use to cool your head. Most of the silent, stern, dignified men I bathed with folded their towels up and placed them, absurdly, upon their heads. When they weren't in the pool, they held the small towels delicately in front of their private parts. I was surprised to see how many of them were circumcised.

In the evening we went for a walk. Chomin no Mori, the people's woods, up the road, was planted with rows of sakura, still in blossom because spring was late this year. In amongst them, larch or birch trees with blazing white bark. A group of Japanese and North American hippies was picnicking among the trees; they had lost their frisbee down a drain. At the top of the path, a bell was set upon a stand: we rang it vigorously to alert the bears to the fact that we were in the woods; they would be waking from hibernation about now. There were banks of frozen snow lying here and there upon the ground. Mayu picked some watercress she found growing beside the forest path. We came to place where enigmatic buildings stood amongst mowed grass lawns, outré pipes and valves: a water pumping facility. There were little old decaying huts in the forest, as if abandoned by the hermits who had once retreated here. Everywhere the sound of running water. We ate the watercress that night, with fern fronds and a flowering plant which Yoshie picked from the land around her house and served in tempura batter. It was called *sansai*,

mountain vegetable, a generic category which includes *taranome* (angelica buds), *fuki* (butterbur), *kogomi* (a fern), and *warabi* (bracken). They can all be picked wild; we often saw people stopped beside the road doing just that. Both fern and flower were delicious, with that wild raw taste you know is doing you good. I washed the meal down with a bottle of light red Chilean wine which Yoshie's boyfriend had dropped off, as a gift for me, that afternoon. It was aromatic, thin, astringent.

Nojiriko

Nojiriko—Lake Nojiri—east of Kurohime, is a heart-shaped caldera in the heart of the mountains. As a teenager Mayu used to walk over here from Yoshie's old house to go to dances at the boatshed. Afterwards she would walk home again, perhaps with a Todd Rundgren song like *All the Children Sing* in her head. American protestant missionaries have been coming here for decades and some of their children were her friends. Yoshie's old house was resumed when the state decided to put a road through her property; but the boatshed, with its faded red-painted walls, was still standing beside the quiet waters of the lake, where families sieved the shallows netting tiny fish; and solitary men sat immobile in high-tech boats with their gleaming fibreglass fishing rods pointing skywards in the still mountain air. Fossilized Naumann elephant teeth were found at Nojiriko in 1948; in the years since, many other fossils have been discovered, including those of elk which, along with moose, bison, horse and giant deer, roamed this landscape during the Pleistocene. There's an annual dig which anyone can join; and cut out iron shapes of the tusked and shaggy mastodon-like beast, a relative of the Asian elephant, have been placed all around the lake shore, each one subtly different from the last. We left the boatshed and drove to the ferry landing, where the buildings had the same feeling of fading glamour as the resort hotels in the mountains. You can cross over to an island upon which there is a shrine; we were going to come back and do that once Mioko arrived but we never did.

Plastic boats with tall prows made in the shape of ducks' heads were available for hire if you wanted to paddle yourself over; I saw a couple of them, improbably, in the top window of an abandoned building. Out on the water they looked antediluvian, more plesiosaur than duck or goose. We drove on around the lake, climbing a steep hill and coming down the other side then taking a turn-off which led, via an alarmingly tight hairpin bend, to a luxurious resort hotel built on a small promontory overlooking the water. Yoshie wanted to have tea here, in a hushed downstairs room where the service was elaborate and mannered and we were the only customers. Disconcertingly, I could smell the waiter's breath as he bent over to place my coffee before me; it wasn't unpleasant, exactly, just odd. Yoshie's boyfriend once owned a section of the lake shore which he gave up so that the hotel could be built here where, it seems, nobody ever comes and where a sense of melancholy was pervasive and without the sweetness sometimes associated with sadness. It settled amongst the bare branches of the birch trees growing outside the tearoom, as a solitary bird alighted and began to repeat its plaintive, lost cry. Yoshie enjoys coming here, she said, because it makes her feel calm. Her boyfriend was going to take her, next week, to see a bee-keeper who sells a honey she likes. She said that one bee, in its entire lifetime, will make just a single teaspoon full of honey; and Mayu teared up. Yoshie's boyfriend also owns a mountain in the hinterland east of here and he told her she could dump anything she no longer needs there. Futons, wooden furniture etc.; though not plastic. In two decades, he said, it will all be gone. He is still farming his land but gave up rice paddy cultivation a couple of years ago because it became too hard for him—the constant bending, I presume. We drove on, past the quiet bay which, in summer, is Mayu and Mioko's swimming place and lunched at a roadhouse between Furuma and Mure where both car park and restaurant were jam packed and the waitresses literally ran from kitchen to table and back again. Ours had improbably thick, curling eye-lashes which resembled, Yoshie remarked, sardonically, those of a horse. She was a slender young woman who seemed somehow to have come here from another decade, the 1950s perhaps.

The onsen was further down the mountain from the one we'd gone to the day before, unassuming in style, somewhat dilapidated. The inside pool was much hotter than the one outside; where you could lie full length and gaze into the branches of a cherry blossom tree in which a bird, a honey-eater, was plundering the flowers for their nectar. Petals fell and drifted to the ground; some of them lay on the surface of the steaming water or gathered in the drains. The snowy slopes of Myoko glistened through a haze of pink in the distance. I could smell pollen in the air. I tried to say this to the amiable man stretched out next to me; but his English was rudimentary and made out of enthusiasm rather than actual words; so we had to settle for smiles and gestures. I saw here how onsen etiquette is flexible; a grey-haired, distinguished looking man 'washed' himself by casually flicking a couple of handfuls of water over his naked torso before getting into the pool. When we got home again we took the rubbish round to the garbage depot to be burnt. It was at the bottom of a steep hill, in a gully of bare scraped earth, with a long low building made of iron and steel and a small wooden office where you did the business. They used to weigh your vehicle before and after and charge you according to the difference in weight; now a system of scheduled visits, tickets and payment is used. That night we ate, among many other dishes, kogomi, curled fronds of fiddlehead fern. It was *oishii*, delicious. Listening to Mayu and Yoshie talk, I wondered why I found it so hard to remember any of the words

in the language? Even the simplest, most commonly used, like *arigato*, thank you; or *itadaki masu*, I shall receive, said as a grace before eating, seemed beyond me. Even *oyasumi*, goodnight.

Cloud came down over the mountain and it rained all through the night. Gentle rain, like a hush falling, and the morning was misty and warm. I woke up early and finished reading *His Bloody Project* by Graeme Macrae Burnet, a fiction purporting to be a documentary account of three killings in the Scottish highlands in 1869. It is set in a small crofting community and I felt as if I were meeting my own ancestors, crofters too, from Ardmair near Ullapool, members of Clan McLeod; though the protagonist in this story was, like the author, a Macrae; and his antagonist a Mackenzie, coevals of my branch of the McLeods; while the locale was south of Ullapool at Culdie near Applecross in the lee of the Isle of Skye. My tooth had fallen out the night before; it was a pre-molar, next to the eye tooth on the left lower jaw; and I had consulted a dentist about it before embarking on our journey. This man, not my regular dentist, was jocular and unconcerned. He took an X-ray, looked at it, then said there was nothing he could do. I was worried about having to have root canal therapy but he said, no, that had already been done, long ago. He said perhaps the tooth was broken. Wouldn't that show up on the X-ray? I asked. No, he said, not necessarily. That'll be $75.00. On his advice I was using a new acquisition, an electric toothbrush. First I felt the top of the tooth go and then, after I retrieved it from my mouth, pulled another piece out by hand; leaving a stump in the gum, with a jagged edge like the rim of a crater for my tongue to explore. The pieces of tooth, which I kept, are brown and misshapen and somehow disappointing: to have spent all that time in my mouth, six decades perhaps, chewing upon innumerable meals, and this is all they amount to? These discoloured bits of dentine? We drove to a nearby drug store to buy, at Mayu's insistence, an anti-infective pain killing cream for the stump tooth — not that there was any pain, just tenderness. It was a relief it was gone: I could chew on both sides of my mouth again.

At the drug store I bought a pair of sunglasses for 1350.00 yen, about fifteen dollars. They are blue and fit tightly to my head; their lenses seem less an obstruction to the light than filters of it. I almost forgot I was wearing them as I drove us in the BMW east and south, past orchards full of flowering peach, apple and cherry trees, towards the old town of Obuse, where we were going to visit a museum dedicated to the works of Katsushika Hokusai. Obuse is a museum town. Last century, when it was dying, an American woman married a local businessman and instigated its revival as a tourist destination: one of those places where you may indulge the illusion of a visit to the past. Mission accomplished, she abandoned her husband and ran off with the chef of a local restaurant; the very place, as it happened, where we ate lunch. She and her lover are said still to live in the town, and to have opened another restaurant; but where it was, no-one knew.

Hokusai

At the Hokusai Museum there was a show of pages excerpted from his *manga*, his pattern books. There were fifteen of these, twelve published while he was still alive, three posthumously. Two large rooms with their walls, and their display cases, full of framed pages of black and white drawings or brushwork paintings from these books, which were meant for sale as pedagogical aids—the master showing his pupils how to draw. The drawings were swift and assured, with a bewildering array of subject matter: octopus invading the cultivated fields, bird, animal and insect studies, instructions as to the way to assemble a flintlock pistol. Waves of the sea, ghosts and demons, dragons flying up in the smoke from the cone of a volcano. Hokusai's connection with Obuse was made towards the end of his long life (1760-1849). A wealthy farmer, businessman and sake brewer, Takai Kozan, met the old artist in Edo and persuaded him to come up to Obuse, where he remained for three or four years in the late 1840s, with Takai Kozan as his pupil as well as his patron. Hokusai's studio burned down in 1839; his metropolitan reputation was fading as younger artists, like Ando Hoshige, usurped his popularity. In Obuse he made a series of beautiful scroll paintings. One of them shows Xu Fu (Jofuku), court sorcerer in Qin Dynasty China, who in 219 BCE came to Japan on the orders of his Emperor, seeking the herb of immortality. He is said to have returned bearing cuttings of the humble mugwort: *yomogi, Artemisia princeps,* used in cooking, to make tea and also as remedy for digestive disorders. Jofuku made a second trip to Japan in 210 BCE, with a fleet of sixty ships and 5000 men and women, including a contingent of archers. From this second voyage, perhaps by design, he never returned. In Japan he is venerated as a god of farming and of medicine; some scholars think he inaugurated the iron age, and was also the founder of the Imperial dynasty, which used Chinese language at its court until about 800 CE. In the portrait Hokusai painted, however, Jofuku is an equivocal figure: his face a smear of paint, a red explosion. Another screen showed the head of a man who had been executed lying on a yellow ground, with the expression on his dying face seeming to fade before your eyes from horror to disbelief to resignation. Threads of blood trickled from his neck like tributaries of forgotten rivers. In the final room of the museum, two massive, heavy wooden vehicles were raised up on pedestals. They were ceremonial floats, drawn by teams of men to shrines during processions in the Kan-machi and Higashi-machi festivals. Each included an interior roof painting by Hokusai, which must have only been glimpsed, as we glimpsed them, by the crowds as the floats passed through the streets; but facsimiles had been made available for gallery goers. They were diptychs, ornate, highly coloured, strange. The Kan-machi float's picture was of *doto*, angry waves, in both their masculine and feminine forms; the one like petals of a chrysanthemum, perhaps; or an hibiscus; the other resembling the lacy tissue of flesh around a sea anemone's mouth parts. The Higashi-machi work showed a twisting dragon on a red ground, also surrounded by waves; and, on the other panel, a phoenix with a golden tail on a dark green ground. They represented, in both iterations, Yin and Yang. Takai Kozan is said to have painted the gorgeous, patterned borders of these pictures.

Yoshie didn't come with us into the museum; she waited outside. She'd been there often before. After lunch we walked, over paths made out of cross-sections of the trunks of chestnut trees, through the old town. I saw a pair of enigmatic wooden chairs placed against a wall. We passed through a private garden, open to the public this festival day. A mossy old stone frog, the size of a child's head, squatted lugubriously upon a rock under the needles of a miniature pine tree. A spray of pink blossom rose against a black wall. The blue alveoli of grape hyacinths, surrounded by green spears of leaves, pushed up out of the volcanic earth. At a temple in the foothills Hokusai had painted another phoenix on the interior roof before the shrine. There were sculptures of toads fighting—or copulating—in the formal ponds outside. Or maybe they were frogs. Inside a man introduced a recorded talk about the painting, in both Japanese and English, but I could not concentrate any more. I had art fatigue: that bemused state of half-unconscious fulfilment looking leads you into; which you have to endure until sleep or dreams or just reflection allow the images to cohere. At the entrance to the temple, on either side of the steps, were two larger than life size figures carved out of wood. They represented 'No' and 'Yes', respectively. 'No' was a giant with his fist clenched and his mouth closed; 'Yes' had his mouth open and his open hand extended, facing downwards. I asked Yoshie to which we should subscribe. She looked momentarily confused then said that, aesthetically, she preferred 'Yes'. I suspect I asked the wrong question.

We didn't go to an onsen, we'd run out of time. Instead, we went shopping. I'd stopped going in to the supermarkets, preferring to wait outside instead, watching the variety of people coming and going, their faces and bodies, their stances and clothes. Perhaps as an effect of looking at the work of Hokusai I'd become

preternaturally aware of visual compositions and saw beauty everywhere: a black bicycle leaning next to a green pillar against an ochre wall; a field of apple blossom, with misty mountains behind, seen through a gap between two bland commercial buildings. Shinano River, also called Chikuma, the river of a thousand bends, boiling white within its bed as we crossed over a high steel bridge.

Mayu ran a bath when we got home. The late afternoon was still, cloudy and warm, the trees seeming to gather, murmuring, closer to the house. The bath, set into the floor, was deep and wide and hot. Akagawa, the red river, ran outside and I could hear the sound of its hissing, chuckling waters coming through the windows. In one of the fir trees a white-cheeked, grey-winged, orange-chested bird alighted. A finch, perhaps. My tongue kept going to the gap in my teeth where the jagged remains were, I felt sure, gradually losing their sharper edges.

Mr T

Mr Yasushi Takeuchi came for dinner, bringing with him a bottle of excellent sake. It was not like drinking a spirit; for the first time, inhaling its fragrance, tasting its intricate flavours, I understood why sake is sometimes called rice wine. The actual wine I'd found in Nagano—Dark Horse, a blended red from Modesto, California—turned out to be oishii too. And the golden kiwi fruit I'd chosen, peeled and sliced for dessert, earned me the inestimable admiration of Yoshie. It was a feast of many dishes, which we ate, not in the tatami room but in the sitting room, where a vase of faded purple irises and pink peonies stood at the end of the table. Mr Takeuchi is a musician who in days gone by had a flourishing career as a writer and producer of pop songs in Tokyo. He was the brains behind a singer called Nori-P (Noriko Sakai) who had

series of hits in the 1980s and 90s; but who was brought down by her inability to resist the temptations success put in her way; and became addicted to amphetamines. Mr T had already taken his pianos and synthesizers and whatnot and relocated here, where he built a studio in his rented house across the road, out of which he works, as a composer and arranger, under the name Black Princess Music. He was flamboyant and charming, with a capacity for enthusiasm that was infectious: when we said we were thinking of visiting the Issa House next day he lit up and said he would certainly come with us! He told us the bears had indeed come down from the mountain—scratch marks were found upon a log not far away from where we rang the bell the other day. Later Yoshie showed us a map where every bear sighting in the last ten years had been logged: an alarming number. They come down, of course, for food. The farmers used to shoot them; now they are tranquillised and relocated back in the mountains.

There was an upset after Mr T left. Mayu and Yoshie went out to see him off and Mayu, in her bare feet, left the porch of the house and walked a little way into the garden with him; for which Yoshie rebuked her sternly; at which point she became upset at being told off for what was, in her mind, an innocent action. There was a long, sometimes acrimonious, discussion about it, in Japanese. I tried to intervene but, without language, it was difficult—if not entirely futile. Before we went to bed, the three of us shared a hug; I was startled, and somehow beguiled, looking into Yoshie's eyes, to see how closely they resemble Mayu's. Next morning Mayu said she thought she'd worked out why her mother got so angry. Behind Mr T's house is another, identical dwelling, in which his estranged wife lives. They no longer have anything to do with each other, not even when their daughter comes to visit. Yoshie thought that if Mr. T's ex-wife saw Mayu's informal farewell to her ex-husband, she might have jumped to the wrong conclusion. Yoshie has to live here; she is friends with both of them and wants it to stay that way.

We drove to Kurohime station to pick Mioko up from the train. Mioko, Mayu's half sister, from Yoshie's second marriage, is tall and slender with a light, carefree air about her. She loves listening to music and in the car sang or hummed along with whatever it was she had playing through her i-phone. At home she listened to Glenn Gould doing Bach's *Goldberg Variations* (both recordings) on a small turntable with built in speakers. I relinquished the wheel of the BMW to her, not without trepidation; as someone who has spent a large part of my life driving for a living, I often find it difficult to remain calm in the passenger seat. However, with Mioko, it was fine. She drove fast and well, with confidence, indeed panache. I didn't have to worry; I could just look out the window.

I'd fallen in love with the landscape: the great white drifts of frozen snow lying amongst trees in the open forest; the streams running noisy with melt; the crows ubiquitous in the fields. Daffodils flowering everywhere; tulips; grape and pink hyacinths; cowslips; snowdrops; dandelions and docks left to grow wild; several kinds of japonica; pink cherry blossom; white magnolia; canola—we sometimes ate the freshly harvested stems and the young yellow flowers. The good black earth showing through the green foliage; and every time we left the house I saw a pair of upside down gumboots someone had left beside a log at a timber-getting place on the other side of Number Three Bridge;

which always made me smile. Further afield, towards Nagano, there were the orchards—grape vines coiling over square upright frames, the height of a man or woman, so they could be harvested from underneath; peach and apple and fruiting cherry, all in blossom. Like the grape vines, the fruit trees were elaborately espaliered. There were alien metal growths, fans and lights and heating elements, on silver poles all through these orchards. In the unfenced fields around the houses, rows of onions, shallots, rhubarb, broccoli, aubergine, capsicum and many other vegetables grew.

Lunch was at a soba (buckwheat) restaurant where they served the noodles cold; you dipped them into a bowl of sauce of the same kind used to accompany tempura; which, incidentally, I learned, probably originated after the Japanese imitated the Portuguese habit of making battered fritters. The dipping sauce contained chunks of roast duck and thick, charred lengths of spring onion; both exceptionally tasty. The onsen, in Takayama village on the slopes of the Hida Mountains, was built in traditional style out of Japanese cedar: a single oblong pool of hot brown mineral water with tall windows looking out over the snowy slopes. I became fascinated by the grain in the thick beams of wood around the pool, in which I saw intricate landscapes, the faces of demons and dragons, birds in flight across a stormy sky. I suppose,

without my glasses, my blurred close vision made me vulnerable to suggestion; but when I said this to Mayu she just laughed and said: *Or else you are becoming delusional again?* I was alone in the pool for most of the time; I could hear, through the wall, the voices of women talking and laughing next door. There was something enticing about that laughter; as there was something salutary about the custom of segregated bathing. I don't, of course, know what it is like in the women's pools; and I never will. Amongst the men, however, a kind of hyper-masculinity prevailed. Those I bathed with, whether they acknowledged me or not, were without exception dignified, calm and gave an impression of proud self-sufficiency. I wanted to be like that too; or at least to appear to be like that.

On our return we took the bottles, cans, metals and so forth to the recycling plant. It was a different facility to the one where rubbish is burned, though similar in form: a belly of bare earth scraped out at the bottom of a valley, to which you descended by a narrow road, with fir and pine trees on the ridge to the right and drifts of frozen snow upon the ground. It was another ticket and pay arrangement and you sorted your own waste into bins for white bottles, for green and other coloured bottles, for brown bottles; places to put lids, caps, aluminium foil or other metallic substances; ranks of defunct household appliances; a big, somehow poignant, pile of broken pots and pans.

That night, in the tatami room, when my feet got too hot, I pulled them out and, stretching my legs along the floor, reclined full length on cushions. Yoshie looked at me and laughed and said: *Tokugawa!* They were of course the clan who ran the military government in Japan from 1600 until 1867; and the Shogun, whoever it might have been (there were fifteen in all) was frequently shown reclining on cushions, like an antique Roman, just the way I was. Every time subsequently I stretched myself out, I became, in my own mind at least, once again a Tokugawa.

Snake and Fish

In the morning, just as we were about to leave for the day's excursion, a fellow came by in a small white truck. It was Muramatsu-san, the architect who designed Yoshie's house; the builder was his brother-in-law and the family maintains both house and garden during the long periods when Yoshie is in Tokyo; in the winter months, snow might drift as high as the eaves. She was showing him the stump of a dead tree with woodpecker holes pecked into it when Mioko gave a sudden cry of alarm and ran—there was a snake coiled in the lee of the stump. Slender, greeny, glistening, about a metre and a half in length, it looked as if it had just shed its skin—which it probably had. It seemed uninterested in us and slid leisurely away into the bear bamboo. I went looking for the old skin—they are thought to bring good luck, especially in money matters—but didn't find it. Yoshie showed me two shed skins she already had. Later she found this one's too, at the base of the tall structure in which the outdoor blinds are stored when not in use. It must have wintered there.

We drove north and west towards the sea, on Highway 18, the old Royal Road that used to bring gold mined on the offshore island of Sado down to the Imperial City of Edo. There were snow mountains on our left as we proceeded through a succession of magnificently engineered road tunnels, all named; the hills became greener as we neared the coast, the trees already in leaf in the warmer maritime clime. The ocean on our right a startling

blue as we ran parallel to the coast for a while before coming out onto the shores of the Sea of Japan at Nou near Itoigawa. The breakwaters, of which there were dozens, were extraordinary: three dimensional concrete shapes of varying kinds piled, randomly it seemed, in long straight reefs out in the sea. Round, square, oblong, spherical, rhomboidal, like practical instructions in the forms of Euclidean geometry. Long-established and well-justified fears of what a typhoon, a hurricane or a tsunami exploding out of the west could do explains these elaborate prophylactics; though I do not know how or indeed if they do, in fact, work.

At a market by the sea people gathered in numbers eating big red crabs out of yellow plastic buckets; each of which was inscribed with the name of the trawler which brought the catch in. Family groups sat on blankets or tarpaulins on the grass or on the concrete beneath the sea wall; excitable children pulled the crabs apart with their hands. They were large, a foot across, and in such profusion it seemed as if the sea, as we know it is not, were inexhaustible. Other groups bore buckets of crabs away to their homes, perhaps, or to some feast they were holding elsewhere. It was a festival of crab-eating, medieval in its avidity, vivacity and strangeness. We lunched, more modestly, in a cafe looking out over the grassy lawns, with their outré sculptures, to the sea. There were bells ringing. I've always been leery of eating crustaceans; but the noodles I ordered came with half a dozen crab legs in the soup and they were delicious: a delicate flavour, a yielding texture. Yoshie had her noodles in a sauce made out of black squid ink; Mayu ordered what she called 'gooey stuff'; while Mioko devoured, with relish, sushi and crab in soup. I allowed myself a beer and went on into the afternoon with a pleasant, mild buzz in my head. Yoshie was here to buy seafood; she and Mioko checked out the numerous stalls adjoining the restaurant, moving slowly through the crowds of shoppers, ignoring the pitches of those who wished to persuade them this or that was what they really wanted; and in the end decided they didn't want anything at all. Yoshie said the quality of what was on offer was not good enough; it was for tourists not for connoisseurs like her. We climbed back in the car and drove for about half an hour north and west to another market outside Joetsu, which she found more to her liking. It was beside the road, in the lee of a cliff where pine and fir trees grew; smaller but just as crowded; the profusion for sale remarkable. Up the back was a big plastic tureen full of miso soup; I drank some from a styrofoam cup while Yoshie and Mioko sampled live Pacific oysters straight from the shell. Many of the fish were unknown to me; when I saw an enormous red, purple and yellow dome of glistening flesh, shaped like a loaf of bread, I had no idea what it was. The head of an octopus, Mayu said. And, yes, I could just see, at the nether end, a mouth or rather a beak protruding from a mouth. Octopus head is sliced thin and eaten as sushi or sashimi; or else sautéed, grilled or roasted. Yoshie bought a measure of small pink prawns which, that night, we peeled and ate raw; the shells and other detritus was boiled to make a broth for breakfast next morning. She also bought some *fugu* skin, which was deep-fried and served in a mustard sauce; while she and Mioko drank sake in which the fins of the same fish, charred above a flame, were placed in the glass—for the aroma. Fugu, puffer fish, is toxic. The body itself, which we did not eat, is sliced thin and served on platters in such a way that you can see the glaze and the design through the transparency of the flesh; eating it is a kind of dare, I suppose, or indulgence in an intoxication which, hopefully, stops short of actual death. Like cocaine, it brings a pleasant numbness to the lips, the tongue and the gums. Fugu cooks are highly trained and regulated; it takes eight years to qualify. The skin of the fugu was, however, almost tasteless and enjoyed, I think, mainly for its texture.

We drove away through the wide flat streets of Joetsu, which has a special relationship with Cowra—there was a Prisoner of War camp here too, where captured Australian and Canadian troops were held. Mayu has visited the memorial for the camp before and would have liked to have gone there again; but felt constrained by the desire of her mother and her sister to shop. Sometimes, when we were alone, she would say the word

shopping in such a way as to make it seem almost like a perversion. Though addiction is perhaps the better word.

The onsen of the day was high up on the slopes of Myoko—the name of a single peak rather than of the whole mountain—at a place which both Mayu and Mioko considered 'dark'. It was: beyond noir, an expression of the kind of revenge that old forgotten used up things wreak upon the people of the present. A locus for resistentialism perhaps. A rickety old hotel in an alpine village whose name, Tsubame, means *swallow*, with drifts of white snow everywhere and a chill in the air. The pool was extremely hot, white water with indefinable bits of something floating in it and big drops of condensation falling from the ceiling. I had to keep hopping out and going to stand at the picture window, looking over a vast landscape to a line of peaks on the other side of the valley: not volcanoes, a spur of the Japanese Alps. I shared the pool with two stern companions who neither addressed nor looked at me; I saw them both later, wearing *yukata*, cotton gowns, shuffling in their wooden sandals to the lift. In the common area, waiting for the others to come out, scanning heritage photographs in an old album, I watched a little old bent over woman using a furled umbrella to align in precise rows the courtesy shoes that sat on the steps before reception.

We returned to Kurohime along a road that wound around the side of the mountain, stopping twice so Mayu could take photographs. The first were of the Arakawa River, which here runs along the border between Nagano and the adjoining Niigata prefecture; flowing north and west before discharging into the Sea of Japan near the city of Tainai in Niigata. It was all white foam, rushing and tumbling in its bed; you could hear it roar when you stood on the concrete bridge and looked down into the turbulent water. Then we stopped at Chomin no Mori, the cherry blossom park just up the road from Yoshie's place. Mayu said she would like to come back and spend a calendar year here some time, documenting the changes in the seasons, the subtle alterations of wind and water, tree and leaf, sky and mountain. When she does, I may be fortunate enough to accompany her. The park was still and quiet, the white of the trunks of the birch trees luminous in the gathering dusk. The mountain Kurohime, the Black Princess, spectral behind.

Later on, after the evening's banquet was over, Mioko and Mayu and I went out onto the road to look at the stars. There were delicate strings of orange party lights flickering on and off on the front and side of Mr T's house—he was celebrating his daughter's return home—and, towards the mountain, two dim white streetlights illuminated a dark road that seemed to lead only into further darkness. I looked up at the constellations of the northern sky, none of which is familiar to me: where, I wondered, was the Great Bear? Or, for that matter, the Little Bear? I thought of the actual bears, waking from hibernation, making their dim way down towards us in quest of berries or honey or even, perhaps, fugu skin.

We went next morning for another walk up to the Chomin no Mori to take more photographs; the trees were beginning to come into leaf, so that a coppery sheen interrupted the gulfs of white or pink as the petals fell and continued to fall; and it seemed to me I had begun to be able to feel the ephemeral joy, and the sadness of its passing, so intrinsic to the sensibility here. Afterwards Mioko held an incense ceremony to honour her father, whose ashes are buried beneath a white blossoming tree down by the banks of the river. It was minimal: the placing of lighted incense sticks in the mossy earth above his grave, a pause in remembrance, a silent prayer.

Thence to the drug store and the gas station, and to a local meat restaurant for lunch. The braised crumbed pork was tender as bread; you cut the steaks into pieces with a knife and ate it with chopsticks. Meanwhile local farmers or workers sat at the bar and drank sake; family groups gathered around low tables on raised platforms; two men ordered beers and one of them smoked several long white tailor made cigarettes while waiting for his food to arrive. It was a long time since I'd seen anyone smoke inside a restaurant.

Little Kyoto of the Snow Country

Mioko drove us to the old city of Iiyama in the mountains to the south-east. Iiyama was a military town: it grew up around Iiyama Castle in the Edo period. The city has around twenty temples, many of them built along a hillside promenade at a place called Atagomachi. We drove slowly down the parallel Street of Buddhist Family Altars, where rows of shops sold gilt accoutrements for the elaborate, garish shrines people set up within their own homes; parked by the railway lines then walked up to a complex which included a tea house, an ice-cream vendor, a restaurant and souvenir stores. Upstairs, on the mezzanine of a paper shop, sheets of paper were laid out for sale. Sometimes called rice paper, it is transparent, soft, flexible and strong and has nothing to do with rice. *Uchiyama washi* is made from the bark of the *kozo* tree, a kind of mulberry; the canes are steamed, the bark is peeled off, cleaned and then laid out across banks of deep snow in the winter months until the sun turns their green to white. The bark is gathered up again, boiled, rinsed and pounded with wooden clubs until the fibres separate. A glue called *neri* is added, along with water, and the material is spread out *just like clouds* in a sink where a rack and a strainer are used to make the actual sheets of paper. These sheets are stacked, pressed and dried upon a vertical drying plate.

After Yoshie finished eating her ice cream we climbed a set of stone steps to the promenade that runs along the side of the hill where pine and cedar and other evergreens grow: this was the track off which the uphill paths to various temples and shrines led; some in a state of dereliction. The last of the temples was the most beautiful: a garden with banks of ancient green moss and tiny delicate maple trees just coming into leaf. You could sit in the stillness and see, across the other side of the valley, the snowy peaks of the Alps. There were dwellings and gardens, growing vegetables and flowers, in amongst the places of worship and pilgrimage. A series of explanatory texts, in Japanese and English, outlined a complex history of religious, political and military intrigues. Of battles and truces, exiles and defeats, triumphs and disasters; of political overlords who provided shelter and

succour for wandering monks; or for poets and painters who had somehow transgressed against the prevailing orthodoxy and sought refuge in the mountains. Along the temple walk we came across several sets of six small stone carved figures set in a row, sometimes with a larger monk-like figure opposite. In one formation all wore orange knitted hats; in another, their faces were weathered and chipped into masks of suffering or world-weariness or pain. The monk was Jizo, who declined Buddha hood until such time as all of the many hells have been emptied. The small statues represent the six realms: Deva, Human, Asura, Animal, Hungry Ghost and Hell. Jizo is the guardian of children, dead and alive, and the patron deity of aborted foetuses. You see statues of him at or near cemeteries and at roadside stations: he looks after travellers too.

As we were coming down from the promenade I saw an iridescent emerald green beetle, a scarab, on the path. Yoshie took a photograph of it then directed me to return it to the garden it had, presumably, come from. She wanted it to be left near water, among greenery. I had no doubt that it was dead but wondered if she perhaps thought otherwise. We communicated well enough without a common language, but there were subtleties, such as this one, which were difficult to elucidate. The scarab looked brilliant, however, glistening on a bed of grey stalks amongst the green grass.

We went to the Kitashiga onsen at the You Resort hotel on the mountain slopes between Iiyama and Nakano: a vast and gloomy turreted brick pile built probably in the 1960s. The foyer was deserted, the rows of courtesy shoes untenanted on the steps, the immaculately suited concierge and his gleaming female assistants remote and courteous at their station to the right; the big picture window showing cherry blossom trees flowering in front of an alpine landscape that looked almost, but not quite, confected. The indoor pool was a green rectangle in a brown room tiled with slate; there were windows at one end which looked out into the flowering branches of the sakura trees. I still recall how exquisitely inside and outside existed in relation to each other; how the windows, full of petals, resembled the eyes of a flower god looking in upon the holy rites of bathing, during which the hot water leaches the toxicity from your flesh and the weariness from your bones. To reach the outside pool you had to dress and cross an open area behind the hotel, skirting the shores of a wide shallow pool upon which the fallen petals lay drifted like snow. When I came out to go down the stairs I saw Yoshie walking slowly around the far side of the pool, heading back towards the hotel. Petals fell constantly from the great bank of flowering trees above and some of them caught in her hair as she went. She looked like a figure from an old tale, making her way out of legend or into exile. The outdoor bath was elaborately landscaped, with great grey stones you could sit upon or lean against; it had views, through pines, past daffodils flowering among the rocks, across the valley. There were small birds harvesting insect life from the bark of the trees; I could hear the laughter of the women from the adjoining pool. Mayu called to me and I called back; again the seductive mystery that segregated bathing enshrines. Their naked unseeable bodies; mine also. I did not know then about the practice called *konyoku onsen*, mixed bathing, which still survives in some parts of Japan; and I do not know if it is naked mixed bathing either. In the reception area outside the onsen I bought from a vending machine a silver can of Orion, Okinawa beer, and drank it in the smoking area where, earlier on, I had watched an older man attended by a younger

woman, probably his mistress, having a post-soak cigarette. There was a sign directing people to the family pool and one small group—man, woman, chubby boy—did go that way.

Frog and Snake

When we went out to the car to take Mioko to catch the train back to Tokyo, she found a small brown frog on the ground next to the passenger side door, scooped it up in her hands and released it onto the bear bamboo where it would be safe from harm. At the station she and Mayu both teared up—they won't see each other for a few months now. Then we stood at the Bye Bye Place and waved to her as the electric train chuntered away south-east towards Nagano. There's a walk that Yoshie likes to go on every year and she hadn't done it yet; so when we got back we took it. It's a spring walk: in winter the snow is too deep; in summer, the grass too high. We crossed Number Three Bridge then turned off into the woods. There was a constant tinkling sound: Yoshie had bear bells attached to her bag. We didn't see any bears; but, not long after we entered the woods, as we walked down a wide path covered with fallen conifer fronds, I saw her left foot come down millimetres away from the head of a brown snake lying there. It was more than a metre long and it did not move. Perhaps still drowsy after coming out of hibernation. There is only one poisonous snake in Japan, a pit viper called *mamushi*; they do live around here but this wasn't one of them. This snake was long and thin, an eater of frogs and mice. Later, after Yoshie looked at the photo I took of it, she decided it was of the same kind as the one we saw by the woodpecker tree, usually just known as a green snake. I was impressed by her lack of fear: she did not seem in the least bit alarmed by the fact that she had nearly trodden on it. Rather she was intrigued, the way she was by the

scarab beetle. The walk continued down narrow paths that ran along the sides of small rushing creeks which looked man-made. There were fallow fields and fields of planted crops. Onions. Sunflowers. Rice. We saw more little brown frogs: they were about the size of a thumb, with glistening skin and the ability to disappear, it seemed, at will, camouflaged by the leaf litter or hiding under the crumbling banks of the creeks while the water went tumbling by. Sometimes we threw flowers into the stream and watched them bob and swirl away. The path came out onto a road which led up to the Chomin no Mori. Yoshie waited in the wayfarer's shelter while Mayu and I walked up through the trees and rang the bear bell again.

The Poet Issa

We went to see the place where the poet Kobayashi Issa (1763-1828) died. It was on Highway 18, the Royal Road, in Kashiwabara. He was born there, a native of Shinano Province, as it then was and, after a peripatetic life, returned to his birthplace to live out his days. His father was a farmer; his mother died when he was still a young child and he was raised by his maternal grandmother. His father re-married a few years later and had another boy; Issa did not get on with his step-mother nor with his step-brother. There were protracted and bitter disputes about the disposition of his father's property. In 1777, aged fourteen, when his grandmother died, Issa left home to study haiku in Edo; and spent the next thirty years wandering up and down the archipelago; before, having at last secured property rights, returning to Kashiwabara around

1815. Monks at the local temple helped negotiate a settlement between him and his half brother and they ended up, in what was perhaps an uneasy truce, building their houses next door to one another on the family land. Nevertheless life continued to be hard for Issa. His first wife, and all three of their children, pre-deceased him; a second marriage was a failure; then, in 1828, his house, and that of his brother next door, burned down. Issa's third wife, a woman half his age, made the storehouse behind the burned down houses habitable and took him there to live. He was already ill and, nine days after the fire, died, apparently of a stroke. It was November and very cold. He was sixty-three years old.

In an irony he would perhaps have appreciated, when Issa died his young wife was pregnant; the child, a daughter, survived; her descendants proliferated and there are now several hundred people named Kobayashi in the local area. One of them, a seventh generation descendant, lives in the rambling house adjoining the intact storeroom and the replica of the poet's house which has been rebuilt in the place where, two hundred years ago, the original once stood. The storeroom had a steep, pitched and thatched roof; the walls were covered in a smooth yellow plaster. There was a single door and a single window, which looked, from within, like a portal of light leading to the beyond into which

the poet's soul had gone; and a sunken hearth, an *irori*, directly opposite the door, with a kettle hung from a high beam over the fireplace. Although it was mild and warm outside, inside you could still feel the winter chill of that long ago November day.

One of the volunteers (they were all old men) waiting in a line outside the replica house gave us a guided tour. It was austere and beautiful, with a more commodious irori, around which half a dozen people could sit on benches or stools to warm themselves; a sitting room, where visitors were entertained; bedrooms with bare wooden floors and sliding screens, all bereft of furniture or indeed of any comfort whatsoever; though who are we to assess what was comfortable, and what not, in the houses of past? There must have been mats on the floor, they must have had cushions.

On our way to the Issa House we had seen a wayfarer, a man with a hat on his head, a pack on his back and three fronds of pampas grass swaying above him as he walked down the Royal Road. They were the local variety, *Miscanthus sinensis*, sometimes called silver or Suzuki grass. Now, on the way to the temple, we saw him again, some kilometres further on down Highway 18, making his way up a gentle incline into the hills, as if he were a reincarnation of a wandering poet from the Edo Period or from some even older era.

The grand temple, where one of the priests brokered the deal between the two half-brothers, was closed. Behind, in a modern glass and steel building, well-appointed, was the Issa Museum.

Yoshie, as she had at the Hokusai Museum, waited outside; inside Mayu, heroically, translated as much as she could of the Japanese language captions to the display; an assembly of plain, sometimes arcane, fact that was overwhelming. Some of Issa's manuscripts were there, including that of *Chichi no Shuen Nikki* or *The Last Days of My Father*. He returned home for a visit in 1801, when his father was taken ill with typhoid fever; the diary, written on the back of sheets of *Saitancho* or New Year's memorandum paper, covers a period of just thirty-five days, details the illness and death of his father and is considered by some to be the Ur text of the so-called I-Novel, a form of confessional literature not unlike, for example, Norwegian Karl Ove Knausgård's *My Struggle*. Next to it was a hand-drawn map of the Japanese archipelago, disposed upon its side, with the west at the top and the east at the bottom; north and south to the right and left respectively. I saw a few maps like this; they were as illuminating as those, in Norman Davies' *Europe: A History*, which show the continent, rotated, as a remote peninsular protruding from the great land mass of Eurasia into the vastness of the Atlantic. Issa's map was beautifully coloured and intricately annotated, noting places where he had learned how to ease his aches and pains with specific herbal remedies; or where he had understood some philosophical concept heretofore opaque to him. He was prolific; there are said to be over 20,000 haiku (Basho wrote 2000). Some charts in the next room gave exhaustive, inadvertently amusing, breakdowns of his subject matter. Issa wrote fifteen haiku on the toad, fifty-four on the snail, ninety about house flies, a similar number on cicadas, over a hundred about fleas; 150 on the mosquito, 200 about frogs, 230 on the firefly. The charts keyed these poems to the progress of seasons, because each of these creatures, and the other birds, animals and plants he wrote about, represented one or other of the months of the year. I've only read a fraction of the 20,000; of those I have, my favourite is probably this one, describing something he must surely one day have seen:

On a branch

floating downriver

a cricket, singing.

The onsen was on the slopes of Myoko at a place called Akakura. Another gloomy hotel, ramshackle and rundown, though apparently its fortunes are changing: they had built new pools since Yoshie was last here so we inspected them first. From the lift we walked together down dim brown corridors until I branched off to look at two men's pools, quite small, very hot, and sepulchral in their windowless claustrophobic steaming yellow darkness. Again I thought of murdered bodies lying face down, leaking clouds of black blood into the water as a noir plot unfolded. It was almost as if I were being asked to write it. There was nobody bathing in the pools and no way I wanted to bathe in them either; when I rejoined Mayu and Yoshie, they felt the same way with respect to those they had seen; so we took the lift down into the bowels of the building and went along more dark passageways, hung with a startling variety of art, mostly bad, until we came to the entrance to the old onsen. It was, in contrast to the gloom of the hotel, a light room with views; a hot sulphurous pool; a spa with jets of heavily chlorinated water; a small outdoor pool that was, unusually, almost as hot as the indoor one was. There was even a children's pool and, after a while, a child splashing in it. I did not stay in very long however—perhaps I was tired of being alone and unsociable in these places? It may be so. There was also the weariness that comes from the enforced silence of one who does not speak the language. When Mayu and Yoshie came out, we walked back along those strange yellow-lit corridors hung with pictures. Mayu and I slowed, looking at the art. Most of it was unremarkable; but amongst the clutter and the bric-a-brac, the ornate vases and the cabinets of Regency porcelain dolls, was one piece that stood out. It was a large rectangular picture, a copy of a screen from the Edo Period, date and artist unknown, showing a war scene: the Battle of Sekigahara, in October, 1600, when the Tokugawa clan defeated their rivals, the Toyotomi, and inaugurated the Shogunate that would last 250 years. The work was Bruegel-esque; richly armoured and decorated men, many on horseback, contended upon a wide plain amongst low green hills. The reds and blacks, the yellows and blues of their banners lay emblazoned upon an ochre ground; if you went up close it was as if you were looking into the very maw of the conflict, where horse-borne warriors wielding great wooden lances pierced the flesh of men writhing bloodily upon the ground; and samurai with their pairs of bladed swords, sharp enough to cut through bone, dismembered then eviscerated fallen foot soldiers.

Both sides in the battle had arquebuses: matchlock weapons reverse engineered on the southern Japanese island of Tanegashima after a Chinese junk carrying Portuguese adventurers blew ashore there in a storm in 1543. The local ruler purchased two of the guns and set a sword smith to copying the mechanisms; a Portuguese blacksmith was brought in a year later to refine techniques of manufacture; and, within ten years, it is estimated there were over 300,000 of the so-called *Tanegashima* abroad in Japan. The Tokugawa may also have had the use of nineteen cannons off the Dutch ship *Liefde* (Love) which had recently sailed into Osaka Bay. There were about 80,000 troops on each side; the Army of the East, the Tokugawa, was outnumbered by the Toyotomi, the Army of the West; but the conflict was decided by strategy not by numbers; at a crucial juncture, a putative ally of the Toyotomi changed sides and entered the battle in support of the Tokugawa and that made all the difference. Casualties were enormous: 32,000 of the Toyotomi are said to have died. Their leaders either committed suicide or fled; their supreme commander was captured a few days later and beheaded. The clan was not just defeated; it was exterminated.

Leaving Kumakura

We cleaned up the house before going in to Kurohime for a lunch of station noodles. You ordered and paid at a machine at one end of the waiting room, were given a ticket, and then a couple of people behind a small counter made whatever it was you had ordered. Delicious, hot noodles; the sound of people slurping filled the room. For some reason Yoshie insisted Mayu wait up by the counter for our order—apparently in case someone else took it by mistake. This was so unlikely to happen that I thought her stress might be a displacement of sorrow at our going. Or, alternatively, perhaps she'd had enough and wanted to see the back of us? It was impossible to tell. It was the Fifth of May, Issa's birthday, and Yoshie was joining a group of friends in order to celebrate it. We had seen preparations for the festivities the day before at the Issa Museum; bouquets of flowers and trestle tables being assembled for outdoor feasts. We said goodbye and when the train came took the suburban line to Nagano, where we transferred to the *Shinkansen*, 'new trunk line', the bullet train for Tokyo. It seemed even faster than the trip up had been, perhaps because we were going downhill—at over 200 kph. The resemblance of the long white train, with its sloping head, to a snake, once it occurred to me, was irresistible. The name bullet train (*dangan ressha*) goes right back to the beginning, in 1939, when the high speed railway network was first mooted. In the fifty-five years since it began, in 1964, ten billion passengers have ridden the rails without a single fatality due to accident or misadventure; although there have of course been suicides.

It was Sunday, Children's Day, the culmination of Golden Week, when families fly the *koinobori*, carp-shaped windsocks which represent their children swimming upstream on their way to becoming dragons soaring heavenwards. People eat *kashiwa-mochi*, sticky rice cakes filled with red bean jam and wrapped in oak leaves; and *chimaki*, sweet rice in iris or bamboo leaf. There was a bicycle race on too. Our taxi crawled past the Diet, an imposing hybrid built of white stone, with a pyramid roof, in 1936. The Japanese architect, Watanabe Fukuzo, based his design on proposals drawn up in the late nineteenth century by two

Germans, Hermann Ende and Wilhelm Böckmann. Many other buildings in government ring, including the Ministry of Justice and the Tokyo District Court, are Germanic in inspiration and / or construction, giving the district a time-lapsed feel; as if the twentieth century wars had never happened. At Yoshie's city flat Mayu re-packed her bags with gifts to give to her friends, while I lounged around drinking Sicilian wine. When the time came to go we took another taxi to the bus station and then a bus to the airport. The overnight flight was, as they say, uneventful. Next morning, after the soft light of the mountains and the cloudy skies and muted colours of Tokyo, outside the terminal in Sydney everything looked harsh and bright and somehow crass as well. No matter, never mind. We were home again.

3

A Map of My Place

for the neighbours

In September 2006 I was evicted from the flat where I'd been living for the past eighteen months; because it had been sold. I was quite upset but before I could look around for a new place I had to go overseas for work; when I came back, on a Sunday night, there was a note under my door from the woman in the flat directly above mine saying her parents had bought her a place and she was moving out and would I like to take over her apartment? Well of course I would. Curiously, she had the same surname as I do, only with the addition of an 's' at the end. I saw her again, years later, when she pulled into the taxi base I drove out of in Haberfield in tears one afternoon after someone side-swiped her car on Parramatta Road. Until I went to view her flat, I don't think I'd ever been up the stairs before; it had exactly the same layout as my one down below; without the massive built-in wardrobes in the bedrooms but with the inestimable luxury of a bath tub in the bathroom. I remember the stairwell, and especially the corners of the high yellow windows halfway up, wreathed in ancient webs. I also remember solving two mysteries. One was the identity of the person I called the Coughing Man—not a man at all, it turned out, but a retired ACDC groupie and biker's moll called Gillian (hard g) who spent half an hour each morning clearing her lungs of the gunk accumulated during the previous day's smoking. She lived in #5, next door to me. And next door to her, across the hallway in #6, was the person I called the Fucking Man and he was indeed a man, a tall handsome young Brazilian whom I hardly saw but heard regularly. Or rather, I heard his girlfriend, or girlfriends, whom I hardly ever saw either, having rhapsodic sex with him. *Come in me! I want you to come in me!* she cried one sultry night. I think what happened next was his apartment, which he rented, was also sold and he had to move on. The first I knew about it was the day I came home to find two old silent people with buckets and mops and brooms cleaning spider webs and leaf litter and other accumulated dust and dirt from the stairwell. They were mute because they were deaf. They were not the new owners, however, but the parents of one them, either the large Irish woman or her husband, a thin, northern Italian with designer glasses called Fabio who was at first thrilled by the quietness of the building, he said, but turned out to be a Noise Nazi almost as bad as, if not worse than, Gillian. Both of them, at different times, called the police on me when I was playing music, not loud, on a Saturday afternoon or a Sunday morning. Taj Mahal, probably; or Little Axe. Or the Be Good Tanyas. When the Irish woman gave birth to a baby boy called Miles it seemed that grace descended upon them; but after a year of blissful quietude they embarked upon a course of controlled crying of remarkable savagery. Some nights the kid cried for so long that he was hiccoughing sobs, as if fitting and about to choke upon his own tears; and still they would not go to him. Despite this atrocity unfolding nightly, Fabio continued to police the neighbourhood, spitting with rage at Josh, the Lebanese clothes designer next door when she had one of her parties and the queens and the rest of them screamed and laughed and played music until dawn. Eventually Fabio's ménage moved on as well, though he still owns the flat, which he rented out to another couple with a child, a daughter this time, a charming and fanciful little girl, Frankie, who used to light up the hallway. Now two young women live there; I thought they might be gay but one of them seems to have acquired a boyfriend. They might still be gay of course. Emma is a Green Activist. As for Gillian, she made such a nuisance of herself, complaining about the noise from the café over the back as well as the music coming from my flat and who knows what else that Lisa, the English woman who owns the flat beneath hers and is a power in the Body Corporate, arranged for her to go into a home around the road which specialises in housing single older women. When Gillian was diagnosed with lung cancer, her husband Russ, who'd been a drummer in a rock 'n' roll band

and later a postie ('letter carrier', the Americans say)—he didn't cohabit with her, he had his own flat in the building next door—breathed a sigh of relief and went back to live with his brother in Madison, Wisconsin. Sharnie was in Gillian's old flat for ages but she's bought a place in Croydon Park and moved out there; I don't know who has it now, only that he drives a late model VW Golf. Once I knew everyone in the building. Lisa moved to the Blue Mountains, Mr and Mrs Long went to Stanmore; when their son married his wife didn't like the apartment so they sold it to a woman who is an events manager and whose boyfriend drives a black Hilux. I think she keeps rabbits. I don't know who the people are in #2 either although I do know the guy's name is Martin. #1, my old flat, was renovated by the new owner and then renovated again by the new new owner, Paula, who works for Qantas and makes jewellery. These days the Body Corporate employs people to clean the common areas of the building at the same time as they mow the lawns. They even wash down the stairs. The spiders the deaf people cleared away never came back again.

Sitting Room

The sitting room has three double wooden-framed four-panelled sash windows looking out over the street and then further into the west. The Venetian blinds were here when I came, in this and in the room next door, which is the larger of the two bedrooms and which I use as a study; but the ones in the study fell down and are now in the laundry down below. The blinds in the sitting room, however, I still use, even though their fins are encrusted with dirt which is mostly the result of tree pollen, petrol dust or muddy rain water blowing in the windows during storms. I've thought of cleaning them but the labour would be immense and I'd have to repeat it at intervals in the future; whereas if I leave them as they are they won't get any worse or not much. The table under the window is where I sit to eat and where I entertain guests, if I have guests. From the

chair at one end I can see out into the street below and watch the passing show. I've been here so long I know most of the locals by sight and many of them to talk to too. I also remember those who aren't here anymore, having shuffled off this mortal coil, or just moved elsewhere, like Gillian into aged care. Alan, who shook with Parkinson's and who I always thought resembled the poet R A K Mason, used to make his way down to the wine shop most afternoons and come back with his canvas over the shoulder bag clinking with specials. He was a stone mason by trade who'd also been a war correspondent and knew Vladimir Tretchikoff in Jakarta in his youth. Or the fellow (I didn't know his name) who'd worked as a mercenary in Rhodesia and walked around with his hands jammed into the pockets of his jeans and his skinny body leaning backwards in a kind of rictus. He never met my eye. You hear bits and pieces rising from the street: one wog boy saying to another: *Look at us, a couple of sad fucks, walking through Summer Hill.* Cosmo, a retired Cossack dancer of Greek ancestry, used to park his big green Rambler Classic out the front and run the motor for twenty minutes or so every few days to keep it in tune. Now Lucy the Florist's grey Hyundai iLoad van parks there and, if it has to move, one of Lucy's sons brings his immaculate black and white Mercedes saloon to act as a place-holder. The van is quite new but filthy and covered in dings; when a branch fell out of the tallowood onto it last winter I went and told Lucy I'd seen it happen and would testify if she wanted to make a claim on the Council for negligence; but she just looked at me. There are apartment buildings either side of this one and over the road as well. Mostly deco, built in the 1930s; or, like this building, slightly later, from the post-war era, perhaps the 1960s. You wonder what was demolished to make way for them. Once I met a man in the street who grew up around here; he was showing his wife where their impromptu cricket pitch had been, leading from the driveway at the side of the building across a dirt road to a grassy space between the Early Childhood Centre where the Pilipino topiarist lives; and the old Undertaker's and Embalmer's building the IT guy has. People come and go constantly from these apartment buildings, on six month or year-long leases: young couples saving up for a deposit perhaps, itinerants with more obscure agendas. Just up the road is a boarding house where single men rent rooms. Ian is tall and thin and wears T shirts, black jeans, leather ankle boots and blue-lensed sun glasses; has false teeth and a loose, rocking walk. He was born with two club feet and endured years of hospitalisations, a series of operations, before he learned to get around on his own. Years of derision and abuse. He's full of stories, most of which culminate in a stand-off during which he gets out his shotgun. Others are about Bill and Tony's, the famous Italian restaurant in East Sydney, where he worked for eleven years. He's a skilled artist who copies imagery from Japanese sources and reproduces in coloured pencil or Indian ink the faces of Samurai, of Kabuki actors, of chrysanthemums or swallows, drawings he'll show you photos of on his phone. He keeps notebooks full of rhyming slang, which he speaks fluently, and acronyms he's invented to describe the various makes and models of cars you see upon the road. Among those who aren't around anymore is Phil Warren, an English man who lived upstairs at Number 4 for a while. He was a song writer, Tin Pan Alley style, whose unachieved ambition was to write something Cliff Richard might sing. And indeed Phil did in his person somewhat resemble Cliff. He used to buy his own uncured rolling tobacco and would occasionally bring some over for a smoke. He fancied Jules, the stylish French woman who runs the Red Door gallery up the road but she couldn't stand him. She thought he was a creep and maybe he was. He told me once, without shame, that he used to go and masturbate beneath the

Brazilian's window when he was fucking his girlfriend. Phil, who had money, sold up and moved to Thornleigh to live with his son; he used to call me every few months for a chat and then one day he said he had some kind of cancer and after that there was just one more call. Whoever built this building also landscaped the plot it stands upon. Hibiscus trees, a bottle brush, camellias, a palm, the people's rosemary, jade trees, even a pomegranate (dead now) and a whole lot of bush rock sculpted into not very interesting shapes around the dry pond. It also has a name, a piece of twisted black lettering on the brick wall below the study window which I've never been able to make out. Blacklock? Blainey? Or is it Baiame? It must have some meaning. Maybe I should go back to the Deeds, maybe the name will be there; and then everything else would fall into place as well.

Balcony

When Moody came round here for the first and only time he called this my Abba balcony; I still don't know exactly what he meant by that but it might have had something to do with the fact that the pediments and the railing continue along the front of the sitting room windows where there's no place to stand or put a pot plant or anything else either: pure façade. This was after Chris and Paulene moved back to Enzed—he'd come around, triumphantly, to show off pictures of the house they'd bought, after years of living and saving in Bondi, in Dunedin. They still live there, I still live here. I mostly grow succulents because they're tolerant of long periods without water and also take on interesting shapes and colours as they seek the sun. The aloe vera, for burns; the jade tree, for grace; the money tree, for prosperity. Lamb's ears for tenderness. Donkey's tail. Others whose names I do not know. The hibiscus, which flowers into pink rosettes, is a Suva Queen. That rock is a piece of quartz I picked up in Bendigo. I used to have a little two seater floral pattern sofa out here but the rain

got into it and the wooden legs rotted and fell off. Then one day I saw outside the medical centre on the corner one of those tall examining beds with an adjustable head rest and a place to put your nose in when lying face down. I think it might be the very one upon which I lay while Doctor Zuo examined my prostate manually with one of his rubber gloved fingers; and did not find there the roughness that is a sign of cancerous growth. Anyway my younger son and I carried it back and you can sit upon it in the sun or lie upon it and read, if you want to, in the afternoon; as he almost always does when he comes to stay. The green metal frog my sister gave me sits on the windowsill that leads into the kitchen; it has a citronella candle inside its belly which, when lit, will keep the mosquitoes away. These days it's so dry we hardly ever get them anymore; though there was one in the bathroom this morning, along with a big silverfish, neither of which I killed. I've tried growing marijuana in pots out there but they didn't thrive, becoming infested with red spider mites which suck the chlorophyll out of the cells of the leaves and make the plant sicken and go yellow and perhaps even die. I first encountered them at Thomas Street in Golden Grove in 1981, nearly forty years ago, and must have carried them with me, or at least their spores, ever since. To Glebe, to Pyrmont, back to Glebe; to Darlinghurst, to Pearl Beach, to Summer Hill. They infected the leaves of the frangi pani tree I had out there too and nearly killed another succulent, the one with the spear shaped leaves and delicate purple flowers. Both are downstairs now, recovered from the infestation with blasts of clean cold winter air. This is also where people go to smoke, either dope or tobacco, or both dope and tobacco. I have a ceramic water jar with a few old dried out stems of banksia flowers in it and that's where you throw your butts. I like sitting out there at night, drinking red wine, gazing into the noir. There's the gothic steeple of St Andrews in the distance; an araucaria; a tall palm which has a spray of flowers upon it and which is trying to put out a viable frond of leaves as well: a daily struggle I observe but can do nothing about. At night the topiarist's garden looks like a Robert Delvaux painting that has come to life, without the naked women but with a white cat; or one of Le Douanier Rousseau's terrarium jungles. A black saloon car parked under the streetlight shines dully in the night, its windows like mirrors or like holes in the darkness. I know there's nothing really sinister about it so why does it look as if it belongs to operatives who have me under surveillance? Men from Canberra? This longing to give significance to what fancy brings is peculiar. I remember one Christmas night, after attending festivities in Randwick, drinking the Green Fairy with other cab drivers, I persuaded myself that I could see cuneiform letters inscribed in the sandstone cladding of the steeple in a place I called, for the purposes of that excursion, Sumer Hil. They painted the whole building a few years ago, that's why the pediments of the balcony are still that hallucinatory white colour. The single capital column too. Before it was pruned a kind of red wasp used to hover among the branches of the

Suva Queen, for what purpose I do not know, nectar perhaps; and there are any number of little skinks living in the cracks among the brickwork. They too encourage the nourishing of illusion, sometimes resembling dinosaurs as they make their way through their lizard Lilliput. *The ant's a centaur in his dragon world.* They come inside too, I found a dead one, limp and cold, in the creases between the cushions on the sofa the other day. Garden cockroaches sneak under the door on hot nights; or, if it is open, fly through in that hectic blundering way which seems random but is perhaps directed, towards the smell of fruit in the fruit bowl perhaps, or some other more arcane scent, some pheromone only a cockroach would be attracted by. I chase them out because if I don't they'll set up shop, either in the kitchen or in the bathroom, and begin to sing the song of generation there; which isn't a bad song to sing, even in the heedless way my balcony sings or I imagine it to sing.

Next Door Window

If you live alone, as I do, you end up spending quite a bit of time at the sink. Several spells a day. Making juice and tea in the morning, breakfast, coffee, lunch, doing the dishes, pouring wine, cooking dinner. Mine has a window above it that looks out at the brick wall of the two storey Deco apartment building next door; you can see the sitting room windows of the top floor flat and also the bathroom window. The green gauze curtain gives the exterior a blurred, hazy, out of focus look, as in a painting by Clarice Beckett. Sometimes I see a bent over figure behind the stippled glass of the bathroom window; my neighbour at her ablutions. I try not to look too much into her sitting room; after all, it's none of my business. And yet however hard you try, or don't try, you still end up knowing things about your neighbours. The ones before

the woman who lives there now, with her daughter April, were a couple about my own age. She knew I was a writer and was effusive if ever we met in the street; while he glowered and spoke not a word. They were something in the arts. Theatre perhaps.

There would always be flowers in a vase on the dresser by their bedroom window, which they kept open. If I went out onto the balcony to smoke, however, a moment or two after I lit up, the sash window would come crashing down. And yet, not long before they left, I found out that he was a smoker too and that accounted for his drained grey pallor. Neighbourhood dynamics are complex and largely unspoken. There's another couple, with two children, a boy and a girl, who live two doors up. Wealthy, they've been renovating for the last two years and have just put a pool in for the kids. When I used to pass her in the street she would always smile and say hello. So would he. But if I met the two of them together, they ignored me. Was I a secret each kept from the other? God knows. A sparky owns the next door building, he is the son of Greek immigrants, he came here when he was three. Sparky does all of the maintenance on the building himself. It's his pride and joy and he has it in pretty good shape. He's a pleasant friendly fellow but you wouldn't want to get on the wrong side of him in a fight. Proprietorial too. Bobbie told me that when she and Elaine lived next door Sparky, whenever he wanted to do something to their flat, would just walk in and do it. I had a Greek landlord like that in Darlinghurst, he would let himself in when he thought we weren't there and sit in the sitting room reading the newspaper. I know this because he did it one Saturday morning when I'd gone out and my girlfriend was still in bed. She stayed there until he left. The woman and her daughter go off each weekday morning on a bicycle, the woman peddling and April sitting up behind in her helmet with her arms around her mother's waist. A couple of months ago I saw them in the street with grazes and bruises and bandages after a cycling accident. The mother's wounds were worse than the daughter's. When they first moved in I used to leave gifts by the letter box for April. I was having a clean-out at the time, getting rid of old keepsakes. I never knew if she received them or not; or, if she did, whether she knew where they came from. I didn't mind; I wanted them to be like magic; and perhaps they were. I sometimes wonder who her father might be—she's young, only six or seven years old—because I've never seen anyone around here who might fit that description. When people see a shot of a lighted window at night, through gauze, with a suggestion of something untoward going on behind the white lace curtains, they generally think of Alfred Hitchcock; but I'm always reminded of the opening scenes of Louis Malle's *Atlantic City*, with Susan Sarandon and Burt Reynolds. He watches her after work ritual—she serves in a fish shop at the casino—washing her naked torso with lemon juice at the sink under the kitchen window in her apartment; later they become involved in a cocaine deal gone wrong. The movie is elegant and tolerant and has an almost happy ending. It isn't so much that you watch as that you notice; then you might watch. Living so close together you become, involuntarily, intimate strangers. Of course I am under the same scrutiny, there must be people around here who have worked out my habits too. Michael, for instance, writer, theatre technician, handyman, who lives over the road. He and his wife Pleasance moved up to the Blue Mountains a few years ago and left the house to their kids; but Michael is back now, looking older and frailer and more determined, while Pleasance, a painter, is still in the mountains. She visits sometimes and looks as he does, only more determined. Michael seems to have decided not to chat with me in the street anymore. A friendly hello and a wave but no more talks. How have I offended? He's a Christian; god knows. To be honest, I often found our talks tedious: so why do I miss them? I was on the deck the other day when the woman and her daughter dismounted from their bicycle and she looked up with a sweetly whimsical, half hopeful look upon her face; but I don't think she saw me.

Study Window

In cities there are places which are lost in time; they disappear and remain invisible until someone comes upon them; they are usually lost again soon afterwards. They are both portals and dead ends; the most reliable indication of their presence is their anonymity. I saw a few of them when I was a taxi driver, usually in the buttery late afternoon light falling on sandstone down the end of some forgotten street; or in a stark black and white-lit cul-de-sac on a dark night. They would appear and open and wait and then they would be gone again. I remember one in the warehouse district in Zetland. It was late and after I dropped off and was turning the car around to go back to the CBD my headlights illuminated a painted sign fading from a brick wall. It showed a pair of 1940s style red high heels;

with the legend *Gay Shoes* inscribed below. Another time I was dropping off in Fig Tree Lane, which runs beneath the west wall of the Waverley Cemetery in Bronte. The wall is made of massive oblong sandstone blocks which, on the night in question, seemed to be oozing gore from the massed graves above. Henry Lawson is buried there; so is Henry Kendall; and Dorothea Mackellar, who wrote *I love a sunburnt country* and was admired by Joseph Conrad (her person, not the poem). Again the visitation, or vastation, happened as I turned the car around. My headlights shone into a garage where a fantastical pair, a man as tall as the wind, a child a quarter his height, both dressed in white, with white faces, turned from their work to look at me. They were taking down, or hanging up, white masks, white puppets, white marionettes, from hooks along the interior walls; and looked like characters out of *Pan's Labyrinth*. I know there must be some rational explanation for this uncanny sight but I have never been able to figure out what it might have been: because of the fear that gripped me, because of the baleful way they looked at me, because, it seemed, they were custodians of the ghosts of the many dead—more than 80,000—buried up above. The third example is more mundane and for that very reason more resonant. I have one out the window of my study. One of those dead ends, I mean, one of those portals. It's in the chimney of Michael and Pleasance's terrace house, made of pale brick with carved zig zag ornaments, a sober crown, and three semi-circular ceramics, like parallel pipes, instead of chimney pots along the top. It's only on certain afternoons that this portal opens, when the westering sun catches on the brick and lights up a path into the time, more than a century ago now, when the terrace was built. When this was a street of boot-makers and grocers, of undertakers and florists, of carpenters and plumbers and stone masons. Of course I like to visit the past as much as anyone else; but there is something even stranger beyond, something unaccountable. It has to do with the clay the bricks are made from; the sandstone that has been carved to make the ornament. The portal opens, courtesy of those grains of sand, of the quartz, the oxides and the organic matter in the clay of the bricks, into an inconceivably ancient time when all of the land upon the earth was gathered in two great masses: the Old Red Sandstone Continent, called Laurasia; and our place, Gondwanaland. There the great Agathis stands; there the flightless Cagou bird roams; there the lizards walk upright upon their hind legs; there croaks the parrot half the height of a man; there the eagle, large enough to carry off any walking bird, flies. I see all of this, more like a vision than a dream, on late afternoons when I swing my chair around and look out the window. There are the heads of two palms behind, a Bangalow and a Tharawal, side by side, green-gold against the glowing sky; and the red tiles of the roof of the apartment building opposite, which is a kind of mirror of this one, with a Juliet balcony made of the same white pillars as my Abba balcony is. Of what use are these portals? Are they not also dead ends? Did I not say so myself? Yes, that's true; but it's also the case that the prism I have hung in front of the cruciform window captures images streaming from this portal and refracts them into the room where I sit, day after day, tapping out words just like these ones which you see before you now. And words themselves, as everyone knows, are portals too: not just to the past but into the future as well. Do you not believe me? Take *tallowood*, the common name for the eucalypt that grows outside the window. Tallow is an ancient word, from Proto-Indo-European **del* which means *flow*. In Middle Irish this becomes *delt*, dew; in Old Armenian, a word for rain. The tallowood, when milled, is greasy to the touch; it is one of the trees upon whose leaves the koala feed; not that there are any of them around here now. Michael and Pleasance, and their fellow residents, fifteen years ago, convinced Council to plant the row of tallowoods that stretches the length of the street. Michael whose chimney opens into the infinite. Who may not know of the portal on his roof; nor of the flows of time which direct my fingers towards the composition of fantasias like this one: of a future, no less than a past, that we make up as we go along. How else are we going to do it?

Bedroom Window

It is an old conceit, as old as *The Odyssey*, based upon a play on words which cannot be reproduced in English. 'Horn' in Greek sounds like 'fulfil'; 'ivory' like 'deceive'. It is Penelope, in conversation with disguised Odysseus, who first makes the distinction. She thinks her dream of the destruction of the suitors is false; but her husband, whom she does not yet recognise, assures her it is true. It came to her through the gates of horn. But, she replies, how are we to know if a dream is false or true? They are always riddles; even if they are sometimes also oracles. But oracles too are riddles: who was the king told by the Pythia at Delphi that if he went to war a great empire would be destroyed? Croesus of Lydia. His own, as it turned out, not that of the Persians. The story is in Herodotus.

Why should we wish to know the future? Will we not know it anyway, in time? All dreams are true, just as they are all also false. What confuses us, while we are in one, is their veracity. Their concise approximation of reality. Not so long ago I dreamed I was in the foyer of a grand theatre, one of those entertainment palaces full of gilt and velvet and plush. Peter Wells, who has died (I knew this in the dream) was there, sitting at a table; we greeted each warmly, hugged, shed a few tears. I noticed that he had a blackened foot, like those you see on the end of the gangrenous leg of a smoker on a cigarette packet health warning. Peter said it wasn't his actual foot but a detachable extra. His spare foot died but he had not. He was living, perfectly happily, in a luxe apartment that opened off the foyer. Later in the dream I found myself in one of a row of beds on the other side of that capacious room. In the bed next to mine was a poet recently diagnosed with cancer. Serie and I have never met but we know each other remotely, as it were, the way people do these days. She took my hand and placed it upon her belly, as if she might be pregnant. Or was that where the tumour grew? I resisted the intimacy of the gesture at the same time as I acquiesced. On my other side was a brutal and violent man. On her other side was Peter, convalescent again. Or in palliative care. A third writer manifested; all I saw was her face; Alexis is senior, indigenous, formidable. We have met several times but never really talked. I said to her how much I like her face. I do. I said how much I enjoyed her latest essay: a lie, or rather a half-truth. I did enjoy that part of it I read but for some reason I did not finish it. How are we to call this dream false? How true? In the dream I believed that Peter hadn't died; but knowledge that he was dead underlay that belief; and, as soon as I awoke, I knew, without a doubt, that he has gone forever. How often do we meet the dead in dreams? My sister my father my mother. Friends and colleagues. You could say the foyer of that old theatre was the anteroom of heaven. You could say, with Albert Wendt, *inside us the dead*. You could say that when we meet the dead in dreams, we are meeting their spirits, which we carry within us. In *The Odyssey* the hero descends into the underworld, makes a sacrifice and, when the twittering ghosts gather round to drink the fresh blood and so take on again, for a moment, corporeal reality, he has to beat them back. He beats his own mother back so that he can find out, from the shade of the blind seer Tiresias, his immediate future. When he does allow his mother to come near, he learns that she has died of grief during his long absence at Troy. He finds out about the disarray in his household, the unremitting siege of his wife Penelope by the suitors; whom he will, in time, and to a man, slaughter. Like an eagle slaughtering geese. As in Penelope's dream. How is this? Do the dead know things the living do not? As if our knowledge were circumscribed by our mortality; as if, once our life is over, we become omniscient. As if we exchange breath for wisdom. Some summers ago, for reasons which remain obscure, I had a series of flying dreams. Half a dozen, maybe more. They were all different and all the same. I would be standing on a slope, looking down into a valley; and, when the mood took me, I would leap into the air and fly, with my arms outstretched like wings, through the blue pellucid air. I remember park-like landscapes miniaturizing below, the tops of trees, silver lines of streams or wide sheets of standing water. It was always the green world: I never flew over a city. The primary sensation was exhilaration. To fly through the air with greatest of ease. To be able to fly! Another constant in these dreams was the advice I gave myself, to be remembered when I woke up: I could fly in real life too. Don't forget that you can fly like this when you are awake, I would tell myself. Remember you can fly! It was melancholy indeed to realise, when I did wake up, that this is not so. Curious, too. The way the dead in dreams insist they are alive. Why, while dreaming of flying, did I think that I could do so waking too? What is it, in real life, which resembles flying in dreams? That's the question. As to the answer, I do not know. It may yet come to me—in a dream. Meanwhile, for want of anything better, here is the usual launching pad of my nightly excursions. Here, in the ochreous light of an early autumn evening, is the place I go to sleep; to sleep, as they say, perchance to dream.

Neighbours' Windows

I was trying to connect my tablet, via Bluetooth, to a new speaker and it was driving me crazy; nothing worked, until Mayu told me that, so long as one device (my phone) was still paired to the speaker, no other device would be able to connect; and so it proved. Meanwhile there was an enticing list of other devices available, whose names I would not know until such time as my tablet recognised them. There were eight of them; one was a television set but it wasn't clear what any of the others were. Just strings of letters and numbers. It seemed a peculiarly intimate means of interacting, at least potentially, with my neighbours. Wouldn't I learn their most cherished secrets? Well, yes, perhaps, but to pair I would need their passwords. And unless I was a cyber criminal, which I am not, I wouldn't be able to get them. Eight devices, apart from my own. There's two other flats on this floor and three down below; there's also next door's sitting room, which is much closer, just a couple of metres of air away from my bedroom window. Bobbie

and Elaine live there, having moved from the building on the other side when the landlord, Sparky, had to let them go because of subsidence and his consequent need to jack the place up again. They were dismayed at first but then elated: they like where they are now much better than they did their old flat. I only became aware of them one dreadful night a few of years ago when, after a fight with my ex-girlfriend, she took my wallet and ran out the door with it. As soon as I realised what she had done I set off after her; and caught up with her outside the medical centre on the corner. She screamed when I laid hold, not violently, of her arm; and in an amazingly short amount of time that brought a number of other people running. One was a drunken English man who elected himself my ex's protector and tried to pick a fight with me so that he could, chivalrously, knock my block off. There were several women who came to her aid as well; among them Bobbie and Elaine. No one doubted for a moment that I was the culprit; it did not occur to any of them that I might have had a genuine grievance. Nor would my ex give back the wallet. Someone called the police and they too took a remarkably short time to arrive. The detective who interviewed me was a burly, bullet-headed, thuggish fellow in a grey suit, extremely intimidating, probably carrying a gun. I told him what happened and in the end did get my wallet back. Emptied of cash, but I didn't care about that. Everything else—licence, bank card, credit card, Medicare card etc.—was there. The occasion of the fight was my ex's accusation that I was having an affair with a friend with whom we had attended a movie premier earlier that evening. In the taxi home she became startling explicit in her imagination of what occurred between us. It was absurd; I've never had sex with a man; and in the end I lost my temper. Hence the fight; and the flight. Some of the history of the night was rehearsed down there on the corner and I remember Elaine saying, in a reflective tone of voice, what's wrong if he did do that? Because she and

Bobbie are a gay couple. Bobbie's a gardener who rides off every morning on her bike to work; Elaine, more reclusive, might have a job as well but if so I don't know what it is. It sounds odd but, after that night, we became friends—sort of. I mostly talk to Bobbie about gardening; and I talk to both of them about their cats. At one stage they had nine but I think they're down to three now. Their old tom, whom they only let out at night, and who used to caterwaul beneath my window, died. Lola, a raggedy old Persian Bobbie loves to distraction, is still around. There's also a tabby called Mumma Cat and a handsome unrelated young blue called Bowie, since shortened (or lengthened) to Boo-Boo; and that might be it. Bowie was found as a kitten sleeping inside the warm motor compartment of a car in Dulwich Hill; he had a mate called Brodie, Mumma Cat's natural son, an adventurous black and white barely out of his adolescence when he was bowled over by a car in the street at nine o'clock one Sunday night. Bobbie heard the impact and came running out but she was too late. She cried for weeks. That's their TV you see shining blue through the window; on weekends they watch movies, with the sound turned up loud, until the wee small hours. I wonder if it's their set that shows up when I try to connect to nearby devices: if it is, and if I could connect, could I then turn it off when I'm trying to sleep? Or at least turn it down. Bluetooth was invented by a couple of Scandinavians towards the end of the last millennium; they called it after an ancient king, Harald 'Bluetooth' Gormsson (c. 958-986), because he was held to have united the kingdoms of Denmark and Norway. The tooth in question was likely black rather than blue: *blár* can also mean blue-black or simply dark-coloured. The Bluetooth logo is a bind rune of his initials, H (ᚼ) and B (ᛒ). Harald is also said to have introduced Christianity to the lands he ruled but that might have been the result of an act of submission rather than one of belief: after he lost a battle against Otto the Great, the German who was Holy Roman Emperor at the time. Interesting, no? If without much real significance. Or not. Don't get me started on WiFi—*wireless fidelity*. Or infidelity, as the case may be.

Bathroom

In the old days, when rental properties were cheaper and more readily available than they are now, we used to have a wish list: bath, fireplace, garden, we would say. We were envisioning a house, clearly, rather than a unit, an apartment or a flat. Yet I have been apartment living now for a decade and a half and that means no garden and no fireplace; unless my raggedy collection of succulents out on the balcony may be called a garden. As I suppose it might. Fireplaces are impossible without chimneys, of course, and there isn't one here; while the buildings either side do both still have chimneys, you never see smoke coming out of them, suggesting that their fireplaces have been boarded up and their chimneys sealed to prevent bird or rodent infestation. I remember in Golden Grove scouring the streets after dark for pallets which I would bring

home and break up and burn in the fireplace at #9. Likewise, I would sometimes find one of those grey, sagging wooden fences around a deserted or derelict property and tear it down and drag the splintery planks home to feed the fire. That doesn't happen anymore. There's just the heater and the bath to provide warmth and animal comfort on cold evenings. For a while I was able to fill the bathtub to the brim with hot water but then the glass inside the cylinder in the laundry down below cracked and the replacement, for reasons I never discovered, probably cost, was half the size of the old one and ran hardly enough water to cover my stretched out and recumbent form; which went cold, it seemed, quicker than thought. Oddly enough, the shower seemed to stay hot for as long as I wanted it to, as if its water came from a different source; which is absurd. When a few years later the small cylinder started delivering brown water to the bath, I managed to persuade the real estate agent to change it for a new and larger one; so that once again I can fill the bath to the brim and luxuriate in it as long as I like; by candle light if I have candles. When I moved in down below there was no bath per se but there was a shub: a green moulded receptacle under the shower which had a plug so that you could fill it up and sit in it. It was alright for children and when my boys were younger and came to stay, they sometimes bathed there; but I hardly ever did. Also down there were a vacuum cleaner and an electric iron left behind by the previous tenant, a gay man, someone said, perhaps a Tasmanian, who died of AIDS or some other dreadful condition which left him wasting away until, skeletal, enormous-eyed, un-resigned, he perished. I still have the pale blue iron and the red and white vacuum cleaner; but who irons clothes anymore? I certainly don't and on the few occasions I did try to use this one, some kind of black deposit on the surface of the iron (melted nylon?) would transfer itself onto the shirt front or the trouser crease, ruining the garment it was meant to perfect. As for the vacuum cleaner, it is a small cylinder on wheels, with a slight resemblance to the robot R2D2 but without the personality; also the gay man, or someone else, filled the receptacle up with some kind of insecticide, probably because it was infested with cockroaches, so that the machine blows sweet sickly air into the apartment while the hose industriously sucks up the dust angels, the fragments of human skin, the bread crumbs and all the other detritus that falls to the floor during the ordinary round of daily life. Quentin Crisp said that housework is unnecessary because after four years the dirt doesn't get any worse; but I have conducted my own experiments and this is not true. Dust is inexorable, it thickens, it accumulates, it drifts, until a vision rises before my eyes of a suffocating cloud which might in the end extinguish my own breath. Even here, at the keyboard, dust falls, though I do not know exactly where it comes from: the walls are painted concrete, the ceilings made of wood or hardboard, also painted: white not the pinkish, mushroom colour of the walls. I wipe the dust away daily and daily it returns. The only other things that were in this flat when I moved up here were six small ribbed glasses in one of the kitchen cupboards. Somehow those glasses have survived unbroken through the years; although one of them does have a chip in the rim that wasn't there before. When I move out of here—it can't be long now—I will leave behind the six unbroken glasses, the fatal iron, and the nauseating vacuum cleaner for the person who comes after me. Though I imagine whoever that is will most likely throw them out immediately. As perhaps I should have done. I remember when my friend Peter Curno saw the dunny for the first time he exclaimed at its pale yellow, dirt-ingrained plastic seat. *It's a long time since I saw one like that,* he said. There's something wrong with the cistern, it overflows, unpredictably, leaving clear pools on the brown tiled floor; until the water slips away down the drain hole under the vanity with its curl-pattern cream covering and mirrored cabinets. Last night, candle light bathing with my beloved, the water in the tub also overflowed and went gurgling down the drain; but she said where she comes from that is a sign of luxury, of indulgence and of sensual pleasure; and so it proved.

'When There Was Dust on the Window at 4 O'Clock'

The adage, *a picture is worth a thousand words*, is of course ambiguous. Its source is usually said to have been an instructional talk given by newspaper editor Arthur Brisbane to the Syracuse Advertising Men's Club in March 1911, as reported in the *Syracuse Post-Standard*: *Use a picture*, Brisbane is said to have said, *it's worth a thousand words*. Later, after the war, when various advertisers (*Printer's Ink*; the *San Antonio Light*) took it up, the adage was alleged to have been adapted from a Chinese proverb: *Hearing something a hundred times isn't as good as seeing it once*. Leonardo da Vinci (*a poet would be dragged to sleep or dead of hunger before being able to describe in words what a painter can show in an instant*), Napoleon Bonaparte (*Un bon croquis vaut mieux qu'un long discours*) and Ivan Turgenev

(a drawing shows me at a glance what it takes a book ten pages to say) have also been quoted as sources or else just as people who at some point said something similar. The ambiguity lies in the fact that the sentence may also be read to mean it is worth

writing a thousand words about a picture; which is the *modus operandi* I am following here. This is not ekphrasis however; or not exactly; for that would mean claiming that random snaps taken on my phone are works of art; which they are not. Or are they? Whatever the case may be, I make no such claim: what I am interested in is the image and especially the suggestiveness of the image. Indeed its ambiguity. Take the silver sheen on the glass of the four square sash window frame above: what does that suggest? Something inchoate, possibly generative? It was the late afternoon light pouring into the room which I was trying to capture; but that is not what the picture shows; or not exactly. Yes, there is that bar of light on the table top; and highlights on the collar of my leather jacket, slung over the back of the chair in the immediate foreground; but the subject of the picture is not what it shows but what it does not. That silver sheen, or screen, becomes a seductive blank upon which any fantasy you like might be projected. Or look at the panel directly to the left of the main one: you would not know, unless you came here and looked (a look is worth a thousand words) that the dark presence at the far left is a wooden carving of unknown provenance which I have affixed with blu-tack to the middle frame of the triptych of windows. It is probably from somewhere in New Guinea and shows a highly abstracted human figure—legs, torso, head, headdress—in a pose that suggests worship or perhaps abjection. Again, at the base of the upper right hand panel, there is a shape which resembles a bird with an elongated neck in the act of bending to feed or to drink. This too is not what it seems. Some time ago, last year perhaps, the state government passed a law which said that all windows in all apartment blocks must be fitted with safety catches so that (when they are in use) the window in question cannot open far enough for a child to fall out of it. That bird's head is in fact a plug of metal on a wire inclining towards a slot into which it may lock; not that I have ever done so, for no children live here and even when they did, my sons were never going to do something as stupid as falling out a window. The literature on ekphrasis (from *ek-* 'out' + *phrazein* 'tell') is, as you might expect, vast and confusing and goes back to the Ancient Greeks: to Plato's theory of forms, for instance. Or, even further, to Homer's description of the Shield of Achilles in *The Iliad*. More interesting to me in the discussions I have read is the concept of *notional ekphrasis*: mental processes such as dreams, thoughts, flights of fancy. Or the description of a work which is in an embryonic state, still forming in the mind. Or an account of the origin of some other work of art, how it came to be made, the circumstances of its creation. Or even an outline of an imaginary, a non-existent work, represented as though it did actually exist. If you look closely at the picture above, for example, you may see in it, as if in a mirror, the ghost of a traffic sign across the road; the ghost of the white fence of the former Early Childhood Centre which the Pilipino topiarist has made into a formal garden; the foliage of the trees outside, in this case a tallowood, which has been mentioned before; and a skinny palm whose botanical name, nor even its common name, I do not know. So if, as I said above, the subject of this picture is what it does not show, what is it that it does not show? What notional ekphrasis is depicted here? These are real questions but there are no real answers to them. David Mackenzie wrote to me to say that he was fascinated by the patina on those window panes. I wrote back and said it was probably the result of tree pollen, blown over decades against the glass outside, congealing and hardening to make a kind of membrane; but that does not explain anything either. I look at that silvery patina and see nothing I can put a name to: as if the act of looking, and of seeing, were an end in itself. As perhaps it is. So the pleasures of looking and of seeing may be the subject of this picture; that is what it shows and at the same time does not show. I could go on but I will not. I have reached my limit of a thousand words.

Empty Chair

The Steve Winwood song *Vacant Chair* features a refrain from the Yoruba: *o-ku nsu-kun no-ko*, he sings, over and over, as the track fades. *The dead are weeping for the dead*. African thought recognises different states of being in the afterlife. The dead do not die so long as they continue to exist in the minds of the living; it is only when all memory of them is gone that they can be said truly to be dead; it is then that they join the ancestors; that is, if they have not already become wandering ghosts, a terrible fate suffered by those whose descendents or coevals have not practised the correct rites of passage. The refrain suggests something other than simple mourning: if the dead are weeping for the dead, what are the living doing? Do the dead weep because another soul has

joined them in their abandonment? African people also allow the possibility of reincarnation and children are often given the name of an ancestor, a grandmother or a grandfather, not because they are that soul reborn—all souls are unique—but because certain traits, whether physical, psychological or otherwise, are held to have returned with the new soul. We are all combinations of traits which have appeared before; but never in this precise constellation. I first heard the song on Steve Winwood's self titled 1977 album; we had a vinyl copy of it and, for a time, played it over and over again. I associate it with the front room of the house at 19 Costley Street in Freeman's Bay where, in the afternoon, the westering sun shone through a small lead light window which had two prisms inserted into it, sending rainbows of light scattering across the white walls and the wooden floor; and especially with Midge Marsden, who put it on every time he came around to see us. I remember him sitting in front of the fireplace with his jeans rolled up and a stainless steel basin of hot water before him, catching the fleas as they hopped towards the warmth of blood or water, cracking them between his thumbnails, while Winwood sang: *When a western man loses his best friend / Many days are spent in years / And without belief he knows his empty grief / Is a name for his own fears.* The friend was Graham Bond, sax and organ player, occultist, sometime drug addict who, in circumstances which remain obscure, died under the wheels of a train at Finsbury Park station in 1974. Nevertheless, the vacant chair might stand for anyone. I mean for any of those who might once have sat in it but now no longer will. My sister, last seen outside the Lido Cinema in Willis Street one June night in 1975. My father, waving goodbye from the covered veranda at Arbor House on Main Street, Greytown on his seventieth birthday in

August 1990. My mother, boarding the train at Woy Woy station in December, 1999, on her way back to Wellington. Alan Brunton, at the dinner table of his house in Brighton Street, Island Bay, one winter's night in the year 2000. Sally Rodwell, fagging with me out the back of the same house six years later. Lud, with his hat on, talking about *The Decline and Fall of the Roman Empire*, in Yagoona in 2002. Glackin, in his red jacket, crossing the road in front of the Falcon to go in to the Rose of Australia in Erskineville one Friday night in 2003. Jim Stevenson, at the launch of *Beyond the Ohlala Mountains* at Waipapa Marae at Auckland University in 2014. Barry Linton, lighting up butts outside Café One2One on Ponsonby Road in February 2018. Anita Narbey, in the Mezze Bar in Durham Street East in March of 2019. Arthur. But the dead are many, who said that? Frank Hardy. *Who even dead, yet hath his mind entire! / This sound came in the dark / First must thou go the road / to hell.* Ezra Pound wrote that, they are the opening lines of Canto XLVII. Dead but with his mind entire. He means Tiresias. The empty chair I picked up in the street one day. I don't know where the cushion came from; it looks like the ones you see in Thai restaurants. The picture itself is taken in the mirror which stands on the other side of the room, giving it that grainy look; the leaves of the tallowood out the window resemble a dusty spider's web; and the chair itself seems animate, as if it might have taken on the personality of the one—or the many—who sat there. I'm not going to name any more names. What's the point. We all know we will join those whispering multitudes one day.

And be remembered for a time by those who knew us before fading away; becoming an ancestor. You can't see it properly but on the shelf to the left of the mirror is a catalogue printed by the National Gallery of Canberra to celebrate the James Turrell retrospective they opened in December 2014. *Colour is Light* it was called. I didn't see the show but have visited the work of his they own, a Skyspace. A pyramid with soft red ochre walls which you enter down a long sloping walkway. Inside, rising from a pool of turquoise water, there's a stupa made out of Victorian basalt. A moonstone in the centre of the floor and an oculus up above. You sit on warmed seats inside the dome, watching the sky's colours turn. You feel both bodied and unbodied. Dead and undead. *O-ku nsu-kun no-ko. The dead are weeping for the dead.*

Acknowledgments

I'd like to thank Mayu Kanamori for showing me how to upload images to the Internet, Leon Narbey for suggesting I write short essays as captions for them and Richard von Sturmer and Amala Wrightson for their companionship. And Mike Johnson, who suggested that the images plus captions might become a book and then made it happen.

www.ingramcontent.com/pod-product-compliance
Lightning Source LLC
Chambersburg PA
CBHW051559010526
44118CB00023B/2748